Tort Law in Brazil

Tort Law in Brazil

Eugênio Battesini
Magnum Eltz
&
Cesar Santolim

This book was originally published as a monograph in the International Encyclopaedia of Laws/Tort Law.

General Editors: Roger Blanpain, Frank Hendrickx
Volume Editor: Ingrid Boone

Wolters Kluwer

Published by:
Kluwer Law International B.V.
PO Box 316
2400 AH Alphen aan den Rijn
The Netherlands
Website: www.wklawbusiness.com

Sold and distributed in North, Central and South America by:
Wolters Kluwer Legal & Regulatory U.S.
7201 McKinney Circle
Frederick, MD 21704
United States of America
Email: customer.service@wolterskluwer.com

Sold and distributed in all other countries by:
Turpin Distribution Services Ltd.
Stratton Business Park
Pegasus Drive, Biggleswade
Bedfordshire SG18 8TQ
United Kingdom
Email: kluwerlaw@turpin-distribution.com

Printed on acid-free paper

ISBN 978-90-411-6932-7

This title is available on www.kluwerlawonline.com

Printed and Bound by CPI Group (UK) Ltd, Croydon, CR0 4YY.

The Authors

Eugênio Battesini was born on June 27, 1964, in the city of Canoas, Rio Grande do Sul, Brazil. Received bachelor's degree in Law in 1987 by the Pontifical Catholic University of Rio Grande do Sul, bachelor's degree in Business Administration in 1991 by the Federal University of Rio Grande do Sul, bachelor's degree in Economics in 1999 by the Federal University of Rio Grande do Sul, specialist in Law of the Economy and Business in 2001 by the Getúlio Vargas Foundation of Rio de Janeiro, Visiting Research Fellow in Law in 2008 by the Columbia University, New York, doctor in Law in 2010 by the Federal University of Rio Grande do Sul, specialist in European Law in 2014 by the University of Rome "Tor Vergata." Professor Battesini is the author of numerous articles and books, highlighting the book "Law and Economics, New Horizons in the Study of Tort Law in Brazil". Received the Robert D. Cooter–Microsoft prize in Law and Economics in 2010. Currently he is professor of Tort Law and Economics and Legal Institutions and Economic Development at the Specialization in Law and Economics of the Federal University of Rio Grande do Sul, activity performed since 2007, and Federal Attorney of the Advocacy-General of Union, activity performed since 1992.

Magnum Koury de Figueiredo Eltz was born in September 6, 1985, in the city of Porto Alegre, Rio Grande do Sul, Brazil. Received bachelor's degree in 2008 by Uniritter, specialist in International and National Environmental Law in 2010 by the Federal University of Rio Grande do Sul, specialist in Law and Economics in 2012 by the Federal University of Rio Grande do Sul and Master in Business Administration in 2016 by the Brazilian Institute of Management and Business. Currently he is a master in Law applicant at Federal University of Rio Grande do Sul, coordinator of the Specialization in Law and Economics of the Federal University of Rio Grande do Sul and the Master in Business and Administration in Environmental Management at the Brazilian Institute of Management and Business.

He is also manager at Eltzdesign – which provides solutions in Building Construction, Law Consultant in Environmental and Private Law.

Cesar Santolim was born in the city of Santo Ângelo, Rio Grande do Sul, Brazil. Received bachelor's degree in Law in 1982 by the Federal University of Rio Grande do Sul, bachelor's degree in Economics in 1984 by the Federal University of Rio Grande do Sul, master in Law in 1993 by the Federal University of Rio Grande do Sul, and doctor in Law in 2004 by the Federal University of Rio Grande do Sul, Visiting Scholar and Adjunct Professor in Law in 2011 by the University of Illinois, and postdoctoral in Law in 2014 by the University of Lisbon. Professor Santolim is the author of numerous articles and books. Currently he is professor of Law at the Federal University of Rio Grande do Sul and Auditor of Court of Auditors of the State of Rio Grande do Sul.

Table of Contents

List of Abbreviations

STF	Federal Supreme Court (Supremo Tribunal Federal)
STJ	Superior Court of Justice (Superior Tribunal de Justiça)
TJRS	Court of Justice of Rio Grande do Sul (Tribunal de Justiça do Rio Grande do Sul)
TST	Superior Court of Labor (Tribunal Superior do Trabalho)

List of Abbreviations

General Introduction

§1. The General Background of the Country

I. Geography

1. Based on total area, Brazil is the fifth largest country in the world, behind Canada, Russia, China, and USA. Brazil is located in the western hemisphere and is composed of 26 contiguous states, the Federal District of Brasilia, and 5,570 municipalities. Brazil consists of 8.515.767.049[1] square kilometers of land and water area and shares land borders in the north with Venezuela, Guyana, Suriname, and the overseas territory of French Guiana; in the northwest with Colombia, in the west with Bolivia and Peru; in the southwest with Argentina and Paraguay and in the south with Uruguay. Many island chains are considered as part of the Brazilian territory, namely: Atol das Rocas, São Pedro, and São Paulo's Archipelago, Fernando de Noronha, Trindade and Martim Vaz. The capital of Brazil is Brasilia, Federal District, with a population of 2.852.372 (data from 2014). On June 2014, Brazil had a population of 202.768.562 inhabitants. The ethnic composition of Brazil is comprised of 47.51% Caucasians, 43.42% Multiracial, 7.52% African Americans, 1% Asians, and 0.42% Native Americans.[2] The main spoken language in Brazil is Portuguese, with about 237 Native American languages active and a small population of Spanish, Italian, German, Dutch, Japanese, Arabic, and Korean speakers.[3]

2. Brazil's large territory comprises different ecosystems, such as the Amazon rainforest, recognized as having the greatest biological diversity in the world,[4] with the Atlantic Forest and the Cerrado, sustaining the greatest biodiversity.[5] In the south, the Araucaria pine forest grows under temperate conditions. The rich wildlife of Brazil reflects the variety of natural habitats. Scientists estimate that the total

1. Data from IBGE (Brazilian Institute for Geographic and Economic Data), available at http://www.ibge.gov.br/home/estatistica/.
2. Data from the 2010 IBGE's Census available at http://www.ibge.gov.br/home/estatistica/.
3. ETHNOLOGUE, Languages of the World. Available at http://www.ethnologue.com/country/br and CENSUS, IBGE. Available at http://censo2010.ibge.gov.br/apps/atlas.
4. MSN. ENCARTA. "Plant and Animal Life." Archived from the original on Oct. 31, 2009. Retrieved Jun. 12, 2008. San Francisco.
5. MSN. ENCARTA. "Environmental Issues." Archived from the original on Oct. 31, 2009. Retrieved 12 Jun. 2008. San Francisco.

number of plant and animal species in Brazil could approach 4 million, mostly invertebrates.

3. As for the animals native to Brazil, the jaguar is a wild animal typical of Brazil, mainly in the Amazon jungle. Larger mammals include carnivores such as pumas, jaguars, ocelots, rare bush dogs, and foxes, and herbivores such as peccaries, tapirs, anteaters, sloths, opossums, and armadillos. Deer are plentiful in the south, and many species of New World monkeys are found in the northern rain forests. Concern for the environment has grown in response to global interest in environmental issues.[6] Brazil's Amazon Basin is home to an extremely diverse array of fish species, including the red-bellied piranha. Despite its reputation as a ferocious freshwater fish, the red-bellied piranha is actually a generally timid scavenger. Biodiversity can contribute to agriculture, livestock, forestry, and fish extraction. However, almost all economically exploited species of plants, such as soybeans and coffee, or animals, such as chickens, are imported from other countries, and the economic use of native species still crawls. In the Brazilian GDP, the forest sector represents just over 1% and fishing 0.4%.

4. Brazil is also part of the Guarani Aquifer, located beneath the surface of Argentina, Brazil, Paraguay, and Uruguay, which is one of the world's largest aquifer systems and is an important source of fresh water. Named after the Guarani people, it covers 1,200,000 square kilometers (460,000 sq. mi), with a volume of about 40,000 cubic kilometers (9,600 cu mi), a thickness of between 50 meters (160 ft.) and 800 meters (2,600 ft.) and a maximum depth of about 1,800 meters (5,900 ft.). It is estimated to contain about 37,000 cubic kilometers (8,900 cu mi) of water (arguably the largest single body of groundwater in the world, although the overall volume of the constituent parts of the Great Artesian Basin is much larger), with a total recharge rate of about 166 km^3/year from precipitation.[7]

5. In the international economic sphere, Brazil is part of the Mercosur, which is a regional integration process, originally instituted by Argentina, Brazil, Paraguay, and Uruguay, and later incorporating Venezuela and Bolivia (in process for adhesion). The goals of the South American Trade Agreement are to create a common ground for trade opportunities and investments focused in the international markets. Its implementation is given by multiple bilateral agreements and annual meetings. The potential of Mercosur, according to the organization itself lies in its territory of

6. MSN. ENCARTA. "Environmental Issues." Archived from the original on Oct. 31, 2009. Retrieved Jun. 12, 2008. San Francisco.
7. See GOMES, et al. Revista Do Departamento de Geografia, 18 (2006) 67-74. "CLASSIFICAÇÃO DAS ÁREAS DE RECARGA DO SISTEMA AQÜÍFERO GUARANI NO BRASIL EM DOMÍNIOS PEDOMORFOAGROCLIMÁTICOS – SUBSÍDIO AOS ESTUDOS DE AVALIAÇÃO DE RISCO DE CONTAMINAÇÃO DAS ÁGUAS SUBTERRÂNEAS." CLASSIFICAÇÃO DAS ÁREAS DE RECARGA DO SISTEMA AQÜÍFERO GUARANI NO BRASIL EM DOMÍNIOS PEDOMORFOAGROCLIMÁTICOS – SUBSÍDIO AOS ESTUDOS DE AVALIAÇÃO DE RISCO DE CONTAMINAÇÃO DAS ÁGUAS (n.d.): n. pag. Oct. 2005. Available at https://www.embrapa.br/busca-de-publicacoes/-/publicacao/15909/classificacao-das-areas-de-recarga-do-sistema-aquifero-guarani-no-brasil-em-dominios-pedomorfoagroclimaticos---subsidios-aos-estudos-de-avaliacao-do-risco-de-contaminacao-das-aguas-subterraneas.

almost 15 million km^2, a great variety of wealth and natural resources and 295 million of population.[8]

6. Brazil is also part of the economic trade organization known as BRICS. BRICS is the acronym for an association of five major emerging national economies: Brazil, Russia, India, China, and South Africa. The grouping was originally known as "BRIC" before the inclusion of South Africa in 2010. The BRICS members are all developing or newly industrialized countries, but they are distinguished by their large, fast-growing economies and significant influence on regional and global affairs; all five are G-20 members. Since 2009, the BRICS nations have met annually at formal summits. Russia currently holds the chair of the BRICS group, and hosted the group's seventh summit in July 2015.

7. As of 2015, the five BRICS countries represent over 3 billion people, or 42% of the world population; all five members are in the top 25 of the world by population, and four are in the top 10. The five nations have a combined nominal GDP of USD 16.039 trillion, equivalent to approximately 20% of the gross world product, and an estimated USD 4 trillion in combined foreign reserves. The BRICS have received both praise and criticism from numerous commentators. Bilateral relations among BRICS nations have mainly been conducted based on non-interference, equality, and mutual benefit (win-win).[9]

II. History

8. The origins of Brazil as an independent state are recent as its discovery in historical perspective, which is attributed to the discovery of the territory by the Portuguese expeditor Pedro Alverez Cabral in 1500.[10] Although the first human activity in Brazilian territory is indicated as far back as 60,000 years ago.[11] Most academics agree that there were persons living in the Americas who originated from Asia and Europe, prior to the discovery and who would be referred to as "Indians" when explorations of the 1400s and 1500s which took place exploring new routes to Asia.[12]

9. In 1534, the Portuguese king D. João III has divided the colonial territory defined by the Tordesilhas treaty of 1494[13] with Spain in XII Capitanies, called Hereditary Capitanies, controlled by selected families, though in 1549 the control system was considered flawed and was extended by the king as he nominated a

8. MERCOSUR. "En pocas palabras." Montevideo. Visited in 2016. Available at www.mercosur.int.
9. See GUTTENBERG, The Sino-Brazilian Principles in a Latin American and BRICS Context: The Case for Comparative Public Budgeting Legal Research. Wisconsin International Law Journal. May 13, 2015. Retrieved Jun. 6, 2015.
10. See BOXER, IMPÉRIO MARÍTIMO PORTUGUÊS – 1415–1825, 2011, São Paulo.
11. See CUNHA, História dos Índios no Brasil, 1992, São Paulo.
12. BRAD SHAW FOUNDATION, "Journey of mankind." Retrieved Nov. 17, 2015 Available at http://www.bradshawfoundation.com/stephenoppenheimer/index.php.
13. See BOXER, IMPÉRIO MARÍTIMO PORTUGUÊS – 1415–182, 2011, São Paulo.

general-governor to the whole territory.[14] The Portuguese have assimilated some native tribes as their own, while other remained enslaved or killed by European diseases, only in the fourteenth century, Africans would be brought as slaves to Brazil to aid sugarcane production which marked the first cane economic cycle, as the first crop production cycle in Brazil.[15] During this period, the Portuguese had ignored the existence of Tordesilhas treaty and expanded their territory in the initiative called "Bandeiras"[16] which led to several wars around the sixteenth and seventeenth centuries with other European countries such as France in the North, the Netherlands in the Northeast, and Spain in the South. By the end of the seventeenth century, the gold discovery[17] has begun a new expansion country-wards called the "Bandeirantes" initiative which caused the Emboabas war between new and old Portuguese colonizers. To guarantee the order, the crown had ordered the crush of any rebellion such as Quilombo dos Palmares[18] (black slaves' rebellion) of Inconfidência Mineira (separatist movement).

10. In the end of the year 1807,[19] Napoleonic forces had entered Portugal, forcing the prince D. João VI to move the crown from Lisbon to Brazil.[20] The coming of the Portuguese court brought Brazil its first institutions such as the Financial Market, a National Bank, and the end of the Monopoly from Portugal for Brazilian imports.[21] In retaliation of his auto-exile, the Portuguese prince has brought on the conquest of French Guiana.[22] With the end of the Peninsular War in Europe, Portugal claimed the return of the Royal Family, but that was not their intention.[23] Thus, the United Kingdom of Brazil and Algarves was created, but the unpleasant surprise for both Portuguese and Brazilians was the Porto Revolution in 1820 and the Pernambucan Independence Revolution in 1817. In 1821 D. João VI returned to Portugal and left his son Pedro I as regent prince of the Kingdom of Brazil.[24]

11. After these facts, Portugal tried to get Brazil back to its colonial position in 1815, which was denied by Brazilians and the prince D. Pedro I who declared the Independence of Brazil from Portugal on September 7th, 1822.[25] On December 1st 1822, the Brazilian Empire was created, but only in 1825 the recognition of its

---

14. *Ibid.*
15. *Ibid.*
16. See HERNANI, Dicionário das Batalhas Brasileiras, 1996, São Paulo.
17. See HOLANDA, CAMPOS & FAUSTO, Boris História geral da civilização brasileira, 1963, São Paulo.
18. *Supra.*
19. See MELLO, Forças Militares no Brasil Colonial, Rio de Janeiro, at 51, 59, 85. Available at http://www.e-papers.com.br/produtos.asp?codigo_produto=1667.
20. See BOXER, IMPÉRIO MARÍTIMO PORTUGUÊS – 1415–1825, 2011, São Paulo.
21. See BARCELLOS & AZEVEDO, Histórias do Mercado de Capitais no Brasil. Introduction by Ney Carvalho, at Xiv, 2011, São Paulo.
22. See BUENO, Brasil Uma História, 2004, São Paulo.
23. See MOSHER, Political Struggle, Ideology, and State Building: Pernambuco and the Construction of Brazil, 1817–1850. 2008 [S.l.]: U of Nebraska Press. Lincoln.
24. See LUSTOSA, D. Pedro I – um herói sem nenhum caráter, 2006, São Paulo.
25. See VIANNA, História do Brasil: período colonial, monarquia e república, 1994, São Paulo.

status independent of Portugal came to be.[26] Brazil's first constitution was promulgated in 1824 accepted by all municipalities of the country. In order to keep the crown in his family, Pedro I went back to Portugal in 1831 and left to his son Pedro II the title of regent prince. During this period, several revolutions came to pass, such as Cabanagem in the North, Malês and Sabinada in the Northeast, and Farroupilha in the South,[27] in the middle of this turmoil, D. Pedro II was nominated Emperor to calm the masses in 1840.[28]

12. After losing the Cisplatin province, which became Uruguay, Brazil won three wars, namely the River Plate War, Uruguay War, and Paraguay war. In 1850 (1),[29] due to economic pressure and the advent of the Bill Aberdeen, Brazil ended slavery in its territory. In 1889, weakened by economic stagnation and clashes with rural and financial oligarchies, the Brazilian Army staged a coup d'état, which brought Brazil to its Republican Era.[30] In 1891, a new constitution was promulgated, making official the Republic of Brazil, though only in 1894 direct elections would be held (only by alphabetized male citizens).[31]

13. During the beginning of the republican period, Brazil had a neutral international position, until the Acrian episode[32] that culminated with the Brazilian participation in World War I.[33] Between 1891 and 1920 internal struggles led to the 1930 revolution that culminated with the defeat of the military occupation and the rise of President Getulio Vargas,[34] which begun his regime as a dictator under emergency state and had under his mandate struggles with São Paulo oligarchies (1932) and communists (1935).[35] In 1938, a new struggle emerged between Vargas and the Integrality Movement (Brazilian Fascist Party). Brazil was considered neutral in World War II[36] until the attack on Brazilian ships in 1942, which led to Brazil sending aid forces to the allies in Europe in 1944. After the end of the World War II, the forces that Vargas sent to Europe came back and articulated a new coup d'état to take him off his position.[37]

26. *Supra.*
27. See PRADO, A Formação das Nações Latino-Americanas; Capítulo 5. O regime monárquico e o estado nacional, 1986, Campinas, at 61 and following.
28. See FAUSTO, História do Brasil, 2012, São Paulo.
29. See LYRA, História de Dom Pedro II (1825–1891): Ascenção (1825–1870) (in Portuguese) 1., 1977, Belo Horizonte; LYRA, História de Dom Pedro II (1825–1891): Fastígio (1870–1880) (in Portuguese) 2., 1977, Belo Horizonte; LYRA, História de Dom Pedro II (1825–1891): Declínio (1880–1891) (in Portuguese) 3., 1977, Belo Horizonte.
30. See PENNA, O progresso da ordem: O florianismo e a construção da República, 2008, Rio de Janeiro, at 59.
31. See LEAL, Coronelismo, Enxada e Voto: o município e o sistema representativo no Brasil, 1949, São Paulo.
32. See RODRIGUEZ, José Honório & Ricardo A.S. Seitenfus. Leda Boechat Rodrigues, História Diplomática do Brasil, 1995, São Paulo.
33. See BARBOSA, A raiz das coisas: o Brasil no mundo, Civilização Brasileira, 2008, São Paulo.
34. See AGGIO, Política e sociedade no Brasil, 1930-1964, Annablume, 2002, São Paulo.
35. See FAUSTO, História do Brasil, 2012, São Paulo.
36. See SEITENFUS, "2.2," A entrada do Brasil na Segunda Guerra Mundial, 2000 Porto Alegre, at 116–168.
37. *Supra.*

14. In 1946, Democracy was restored with the election of Eurico Gaspar Dutra as president. Re-elected in 1950, Vargas tragically committed suicide after an intense political crisis.[38] In 1955, Jucelino Kubitshek was elected with a conciliator position with political opposers, which helped him make his government free of major crises and to raise the economic and industrial sectors. However, his main achievement as President was the Building of Brasilia, the new capital of the country.[39] His successor was Jânio Quadros, who renounced the Presidential role in 1961, leaving the position to his vice-president João Goulart who was deposed by a military coup in 1964 due to the left-wing positions of the president.

15. The new regime was supposed to be transitory, but would end only in 1985.[40] The Military Dictatorship in Brazil was market by violence, censorship, and repression and torture to left-winged politicians and students; though was also known by the "economic miracle" in the 1970s that led to economic prosperity during the regime. Pressured by many left-winged revolts, the regime passed the amnesty act in 1979 and after the movement "Diretas Já" (direct vote now) the new Democracy was born in 1985.[41]

16. Tancredo Neves was the first president elected, but due a severe medical condition, he did not get to his position, letting to his vice-president José Sarney the role of the first democratic president of Brazil after the Military period. Many economic crises and monetary issues led to the election of the brand new candidate Fernando Collor de Mello[42] in 1989 who was deposed in 1992 by the first Impeachment in the history of Brazil due financial scandals, the role was then filled by its vice-president Itamar Franco who was known for the implementation along with the Minister Fernando Henrique Cardoso of the successful Real Economic Plan, which introduced the Real currency, used to date. The new plan led to Fernando Henrique Cardoso's election in 1994, which marked a new economic stability in Brazil and the beginning of the Privatization process in many state companies in fields like communication, electricity, and mineral exploration.[43]

17. The success of his first mandate led to his re-election in 1998, but the second mandate had been plundered by a large social inequality which led to the election of Luiz Inácio Lula da Silva in 2002 who had a left-winged agenda and started many social programs in Brazil, implementing public scholarships for private education, basic food aid for students and their families, and a large-scale housing program. His popularity guaranteed the 2006 re-election and made for a clean sweep in the election of his political successor Dilma Rousseff, the first woman elected as

38. See BUENO, Brasil uma História, 2004, São Paulo.
39. See SKIDMORE, História Geral, 2003, Recife.
40. See GASPARI, A ditadura escancarada, 2002, São Paulo.
41. See MENDONÇA, Daniel, Tancredo Neves – Da Distensão à Nova República, 2004, Santa Cruz do Sul.
42. See PAIVA, Era outra história: política social do governo Itamar Franco 1992–1994, 2009, Juiz de Fora.
43. See FAUSTO and DEVOTO, História do Brasil, 2004. São Paulo.

President of Brazil in 2010,[44] though her first mandate has shown impacts on economy of the many social projects sustained by her party, which led to protests in 2013 under the reduction of transport fee's flag,[45] the social aid was enough to guarantee her re-election in 2014 promising new economic reforms and sustaining the social programs implemented earlier. The second Government of Dilma would be hard on the Presidency, as many protests, in addition to the growing economic crisis lead to the controversial Impeachment process initiated by the Deputy's Chamber at the end of 2015.[46] Between scandals of corruption exposed by the media and the Federal Courts, the largest protest in the history of Brazil has been made to reinforce the popular claim for the President's dismissal.[47] On April 17, 2016, the Deputy's Chamber voted for the Dismissal of Dilma,[48] leading to the historic defeat on the Senate and the legal provisory dismissal of the President Dilma for 180 days until the definitive vote of the Senate due in September 2016.[49] Meanwhile, the vice-president Michel Temer is the new President of Brazil, representing a change of political standards, from a long left-wing Government started by Luis Inácio Lula da Silva to a right-wing Government led by the PMDB party.

III. Political System

18. The Federal Constitution of Brazil, states in its 1st Article that:

> the Federative Republic of Brazil is formed by the insoluble union of the Federated States and Municipalities as the Federal District and it's constituted as a Democratic State of Law founded by Sovereignty, Citizenship, the Dignity of the Human Person, the Social Values of Work and Free Initiative, and the Political Pluralism.[50]

19. Brazil is a Federated Republic, represented by the Union of the 26 contiguous states and the Federal District, Brasilia. The political system is Presidential with democratic representation. The power within the Union is represented by the President who is the Chief of the State and represents of Brazilian Diplomacy. The

44. UOL, "Jornais Internacionais destacam a vitória de Dilma" http://eleicoes.uol.com.br/2010/ultimas-noticias/2010/10/31/jornais-internacionais-destacam-a-vitoria-de-dilma.jhtm.
45. PORTAL TERRA Governo brasileiro é pressionado por históricos protestos. Visited in Jun. 25, 2013. Available at http://noticias.terra.com.br/brasil/governo-brasileiro-e-pressionado-por-historicos-protestos,f614e49fccf5f310VgnCLD2000000ec6eb0aRCRD.html.
46. FOLHA, "Cunha deflagra processo de impechment contra Dilma." Available at http://www1.folha.uol.com.br/poder/2015/12/1714133-cunha-deflara-processo-de-impeachment-contra-dlma.shtml.
47. G1. "Manifestações contra o Governo Dilma ocorrem pelo País." Available at http://g1.globo.com/politica/noticia/2016/03/manifestacoes-contra-governo-dilma-ocorrem-pelo-pais.html.
48. TERRA, "Derrota na Câmara deixa governo Dilma mais perto do fim." Available at http://noticias.terra.com.br/brasil/derrota-na-camara-deixa-governo-dilma-mais-perto-do-fim,10cf69a55c005088ab079943bfe785a4qa8lwiak.html.
49. GLOBO, "Processo de Impeachment é aberto e Dilma é afastada por até 180 dias." Available at http://g1.globo.com/politica/processo-de-impeachment-de-dilma/noticia/2016/05/processo-de-impeachment-e-aberto-e-dilma-e-afastada-por-ate-180-dias.html.
50. BRAZIL, Federal Constitution of 1988, Brazilian Congress – 1988. Available at http://www.planalto.gov.br/ccivil_03/Constituicao/Constituicao.htm.

States are considered to have autonomy guaranteed by the Constitution and have the power to make their own Constitutions, as they are considered independent Municipalities, which have the power to promulgate their own laws and guidelines.

20. The Presidential regime states that the Chief of State and Chief of Government roles are attributed to the President of the Republic. The Republican system in Brazil guarantees the President to be elected by direct, universal, and obligatory vote by limited time, remaining in power for only two consecutive mandates. Finally, the Democratic regime gives the people the power to elect the President, the Parliamentarians, and to directly act in Brazilian politics through Plebiscites, Referendums, and Popular Initiatives.

21. According to the Economist Democracy Index, Brazil has a high performance on electoral pluralism (9.5) and civil liberties (9.1).[51] As it had an above average government functionality (7.5). Though it has inferior performance on Political Participation (5.0) and culture (4.3), according to 2012 data.[52]

22. The Article 2 of the Federal Constitution states the Powers of the Union are supplementary and independent from each other and harmonic, composed of the Legislative, the Executive, and the Judiciary. The executive chief of State is the President of the Republic, elected by direct vote to a four years' mandate, which can be extended by more four years through re-election. In the Federated States, the Executive is represented by Governors and in the Municipalities by Mayors. The Legislative powers are concentrated in the Union by the National Congress, which is bicameral, divided by the Deputies Chamber (representing the people's interests) and the Senate (representing the states' interests) for a mandate of four years. The Deputies Chamber is composed by a proportional ratio of representatives according to the State's population, as the Senate is composed by three Senators for each state who have a mandate of eight years. In the Federated States, the Legislative is represented by the State Assemblies and in Municipalities by the County Chambers.[53] Finally, the different Courts in Brazil represent the Judiciary. In the Federated States, it is composed of the State Courts formed by local Forums of Primary Judges and State Courts formed by Groups of Senior Judges; in the Union, by the Federal Justice and Federal Courts and in the High Court level by the Superior Justice Court and the Supreme Federal Court; along with the Labor Justice represented by the Labor Judges, Regional Courts, and the Superior Labor Court. The Judges are not elected in Brazil, their selection is by Public Selections based on their Legal Careers and Performance on Tests in the case of lower courts and by the Nomination by their Peers in State, Federal, and Labor Courts and by the Executive in the Higher Courts.

51. THE ECONOMIST. Democracy Index Economist Intelligence Unit. 2010. Visited in Jun. 21, 2013. Available at http://www.eiu.com/home.aspx#introduction.
52. THE ECONOMIST. Democracy Index Economist Intelligence Unit. 2012. Visited in Jun. 21, 2013. Available at http://www.eiu.com/home.aspx#introduction.
53. Adapted from the text of WIKIPEDIA, The Free Encyclopedia. Available at: http://pt.wikipedia.org/wiki/Pol%C3%ADtica_do_Brasil.

23. The Article 3 of the Constitution states that the fundamental objectives of the Republic is to: build a free, just, and solidary society; guarantee national development; eradicate poverty and marginalization, and reduce social and regional inequalities; promote welfare of all, without prejudice of origin, race, gender, color, age, or any discrimination.

24. As for the international relations, Brazil has elected the following principles in Article 4: national independence, human rights primacy, self-determination of the nations, non-intervention, state equity, peace defense, pacific conflict solution, rejection of terrorism and racism, cooperation between nations for the progress of humankind, and political asylum concession. In addition, its paragraph includes that Brazil will seek the economic, political, social, and cultural integration of the nations of Latin America, aiming to formulate a Latin American community of nations.

IV. Economic and Social Values

25. Brazil is a country that still depends mostly on the wealth generated by its Agriculture and Meat production sectors, though it has shown nascent activities in both the Manufacturing and Services sectors. Historically, the economy of Brazil started mostly with the extraction of its natural wealth trough the exportation of Wood, Gold, and Rubber to Portugal as part of the Colonial Pact. As Brazil became an Empire of its own, industry was still not present, as the Oligarchies became the main source of wealth, exporting Milk and Coffee worldwide. During the second Reign, Pedro II brought innovations such as the train and the telegraph to Brazil, starting a fever of novelties and an urge for industrialization, but it was only after the 1930s Revolution that Getúlio Vargas would invest in the real Brazilian Industry, which would reach its peak during the Military Dictatorship, especially during the 1970s. Nowadays, Brazilian Economy is still Agro-based though some efforts to bring innovation is being made, the institutions of the country still struggle to get Industry on its feet.[54]

26. The Brazilian current Economic and Social Values can be found in the Brazilian Federal Constitution, which states in its Article 170, the "general principals of the economic activity," in the Article 193 the guidelines of the "Social Order," and in a spread of articles about the tributary function, health care system, and social aid.[55]

27. The Article 170 states as the general principles of the economic activity: "the national sovereignty, the private ownership, the social function of property, the free market, consumer protection, the environment protection and different treatment

54. See FILIPPI, Evolução econômica e institucional do setor primário no Brasil: em direção ao desenvolvimento rural?, 2006, Maputo.
55. (1) BRAZIL, Federal Constitution. Available at http://www.planalto.gov.br/ccivil_03/Constituicao/Constituicao.htm.

according to the impact of product and services and its production and elaboration processes; the reduction of regional and social inequities; the full employment goal seeking; and the special treatment to small corporations with residence and administration in the country." Its paragraph states that "is secured to all the free exercise of any economic activity, independently of public authorization, except cases predicted by law."

28. In addition, Article 5, which states the fundamental rights of Brazil (not revocable by constitution amendments), guarantees the general principles of:

> equality, liberty, security and property, adding to: the freedom of speech, privacy, inviolability of the private property (except in flagrant or disaster to give aid or by legal order during the day); the mail security; the free exercise of work, craft or profession on the terms of the law; the free access to information; the free locomotion in the national territory during times of peace; the freedom of reunion; the freedom of association (except for para-military purposes); the social function of the property; the protection of the private property and retribution for public expropriation; the damages payment for public use of private property; the protection of the small rural area for debit payment purposes; the protection of the author's rights, the intellectual property; the inheritance; the defense of the consumer; and finally, the rule of law.

29. In the agribusiness sector, the Article 184 states, "the Agriculture and Meat production must accomplish their social function; otherwise the government will expropriate the land to fulfil its function defined by law." This article shows not only that the land distribution of Brazil is a concerning of the Government, but also shows that the private property is not fully protected by any use of their proprietors. Which endorses the goals of the Brazilian government to generate employments and optimally use the lands within the country. On the other hand, the void concept of "social function" gives a lack of protection to the producers, which can be deprived of their lands from the administration given their own interpretation of "social function."

30. The financial market in Brazil is a complex phenomenon. Starting with the Royal Family from Portugal fleeing to Brazil and opening the first "Bank of Brazil" and its bankruptcy during the First Reign to the opening of the second "Bank of Brazil" from the former "Bank Mauá" and the opening of the financial Market during the 1990s to foreign banks. Nowadays, Brazil counts with many big Banks, though smaller banks are responsible for the main financial operations, called "micro-credit" investments to fulfill the market need to get the "new middle class" promoted by the Luiz Inácio Lula da Silva and Dilma Rousseff governments. The constitution of Brazil defines in Article 192 that the national financial system is structured to promote the equilibrated development of the Country and to serve the collective interests, including the credit cooperatives. Though the financial market is responsible for Brazilian development in the latest years due the ascending of the new middle class, many struggles are being made due the ultra-bankruptcy of the same new middle class, which causes turmoil's on the directions that Brazilian economy is taking in the second mandate of Dilma Rousseff.

31. The title VIII of the Brazilian Constitution deals with the Social Order and in its Article 193 states, "the social order has its base on work and its goal is the welfare and social justice." The Article 194 defines the Social Security as an integrated action package given by the Society and the State aimed to secure rights of health care, retirement, and social assistance. The paragraph of the Article 194 elect the following principles for this purpose: universal covering on services; uniformity and equivalence of benefits and services between rural and urban population; selectivity and distribution of benefits and services giving; non-reduction of benefits; equity in the distribution of costs; diversity in the financial base; democratic character and decentralization of the administration through an quasi-management with the participation of workers, employers, retired, and the government in plural offices.

32. In section II of this chapter, the Article 196 establishes that the health care system is a right of everyone and a duty of the State, granted through social and economic policies aimed to reduce the risks of sickness and other illnesses and the universal and equal access to actions and services to protect, promote, and recover health. The Uniform Health System (Sistema Único de Saúde – SUS) is defined in Article 198 as a network regional-wide constituted in the following principles: decentralization, with a single director in each state division; integral service, with priority for preventive actions without let any providential service aside; community participation.

33. Article 201 establishes the public security system, which is organized under a central regime with contributive character and mandatory affiliation, observed criteria that preserve the financial and actuarial equilibria and will cover: events of sickness, handicap, death, and aging; protection to motherhood, especially to the pregnancy period; protection to the worker and unintended unemployed; family-salary and reclusion-aid for dependents of low income secured; pension for death to companion and dependents.

34. The section IV established the social care system which will be extended to whoever needs, independent of social security contribution and aims to: protect the institution of the family, motherhood, childhood, teenage, and the aging process; to aid children and teenagers in need; promote the integration to the work market; to habilitate and re-habilitate people with disability and to re-introduce them to their community and finally, to guarantee an minimum wage to whoever has a disability or an elder who can prove to not have means to sustain themselves or have it through their families according to the law.

35. The Chapter 2 of the Brazilian Constitution indicates the social rights to be protected by the State. In its Article 6 are stated the social rights: the education, health care, feeding, work, housing, leisure, security, social security, the motherhood and childhood protection, and the assistance to those in need.

36. Article 7 defines the rights of the urban and rural workers to sustain their social condition as: the protection against arbitrary or unjust dismissal which will require compensatory damages and other rights defined by law; the unemployment insurance; warranty fund by length of service; minimum wage established by law that is capable of addressing vital and basic needs such as family's housing; feeding; education; health; leisure; clothing; hygiene; transportation; and social security with periodic adjustments that can preserve one's acquisitive power. A minimum wage proportional to the extension and complexity required by work; irreducibility of wages, except through class agreements; prohibition of wages under the legal minimum wage; one-third wage based on the full remuneration or retirement wage; night-wage superior to daytime wages; legal punishment for retaining of wages; participation on profits or results not attached to remuneration and exceptionally participation in the corporation management as defined by law; family-wage paid to dependents of low income by terms of law; journey of work not more than 8 hours a day and 44 weekly hours, the compensation of hours possible through class agreements; journey of 6 hours for non-stop turns, except if negotiated in class agreements; weekly paid days off, preferable on Sundays. Wages of work overtime superior to 50% of the regular worker wage; Annual vacations with at least one third of regular wages in addition to the periods salary; Motherhood license without wage and working status changing of 120 days; Fatherhood license on the terms given by the law; Protection of women work market, throughout specific incentives in the terms given by the law; Prior notice proportional to the time of service, with the minimum fixed in thirty days; Reduction of the risks related to work, through health, hygiene and security laws; Additional wage to hazardous, dangerous or unhealthy activities; Retirement. Free assistance to children and dependents from the birth up to five years of age in kindergarten and preschools. Recognition of conventions and collective bargains of work; Protection to the automatization process; Work liability insurance paid by the employer not excluding damages due negligence or intent. Lawsuits for working related credits with limitation period of five years to urban and rural workers after two years from the working contract extinction; Prohibition of salary distinction by sex, age, color or civil status; Prohibition of any discrimination of salary and admission criteria to deficient persons. Prohibition of the distinction of manual, technical, and intellectual works and workers. Prohibition of night shifts, dangerous, or unhealthy works for workers below the age of 18 or any night shift for workers under the age of 16, except as an apprentice of at least 14 years. Equal rights between the worker and eventual servant. The paragraph adds that:

> the domestic workers have the same rights predicted in IV, VI, VII, VIII, X, XIII, XV, XVI, XVII, XVIII, XIX, XXI, XXII, XXIV, XXVI, XXX, XXXI and XXXIII and simplification of tributary obligations predicted in I, II, III, IX, XII, XXV and XXVIII, as integration to the social security system.

37. The Article 8 by its turn, states that the professional and syndicate association is free, observing that the law cannot require the State authorization for an

Syndicate foundation, except that it register with the competent agency, and is forbidden for the State to interfere in the Syndicate organization; More than one Syndicate to an economic or professional category in the same territory is forbidden, which will be defined by the interested workers and employers, the minimum influence territory of a County. The syndicate will promote the defense of collective and individual rights of the category in legal and administrative questions; the main assembly will state the contribution which will be plaid in source to sustain the syndicate representation, independent of the contribution predicted in law; Nobody is obligated to adhere or remain as a part to a syndicate; The participation of syndicates in collective negotiations of work are mandatory; The retired worker has the right to vote or to be voted in syndicate organizations; Is forbidden the dispense of an employee part of a syndicate from the application to direction or representation of the syndicate to one year after the mandate, except if the employee incur in severe fault in the terms given by the law; the paragraph of this article states that its content is applied to rural syndicates and fishing organizations.

38. The Article 9 secures the right of strikes to defend worker's interests, except essential activities or abusive behavior. In addition, the Article 10 secures the participation of workers and employers in the public branches that are related to their professional and jubilation interests. Finally, the Article 11 states that in corporations with more than 200 employees it is secured elections for one representative of these to promote direct negotiations with the employer.

39. In order to sustain the State and its Social Security System, Brazil has a list of Taxes and Fees provided by the Constitution and defined by the Law. The Article 153 states that the Union taxes will cover: the importation of alien products; the exportation to the foreign of national of nationalized products; the income of any nature; the manufactured products; credit, exchange and insurance or related to titles and mobiliary currencies; the rural property; the great fortunes in terms of complementary law. For the federated states, the Article 155 defines their taxes to cover transmission of values through death and donation of any wealth or rights; operations related to circulation of goods and transportation services between states and municipalities and communication, even though their origin is traced to alien countries; vehicle property. Finally, the Article 156 establishes that the Municipalities can collect taxes based on: the urban property; the transmission between living person of any title by trade act of real state, except warranties and cessation of powers to its acquisition. The constitution adds to the receipt of the federated states the restitution of taxes given to the Union by their autarchies and foundations by them maintained and 20% of the taxes acquired by the Union referring to Article 154, I. As for the Municipalities, the Article 158 adds to their receipts the product of their collection of income taxes from their autarchies and foundations sustained by them. The taxes used as the receipt utilization are given by the Executive power through the plurennial plan, the budged directions and the annual budged that will be reviewed by the congress according to Article 165 and paragraphs of the Constitution.

§2. Legal Systems

I. Primacy of Legislation and Codification

40. Brazilian Law is considered part of the Civil Law legal systems. The Roman-German tradition, as opposed to Common Law systems, where the rules are consequences of tradition, customs, and jurisprudence, with a few legal statements; Civil Law, works under law making processes directly from social costumes to Legislations which dictates the current norms through a large content in the Federal Constitution, Federal Laws, State Laws, and Municipalities Laws. According CANOTILHO "the Brazilian Constitution was able to rise to the role of fundamental legal rule."[56] In fact, "the Bill of 1988 is what might be called an analytical and overloaded constitution."[57] So, there is a large number of issues that are not normally found in constitutional texts, but that are present in the Brazilian Constitution, including some aspects of liability, and torts (e.g., public liability, Article 37, §6º; judicial liability, Article 5º, LXXV; employers' liability, Article 7º, XXVIII; liability for radioactive damages, Article 21, XXIII, "c;" environmental damages, Article 225, §3º; moral damages, Article 5º, V e X). Besides that, the Constitution is the supreme law in Brazil, which supersedes all and any other rules, whether statutory or other.

41. Regarding Private Law, its competence is usually Federal. Usually Private Law and Commercial Law are regulated under Federal Laws, though both Federal and State Laws regulate Consumer Law, even though its guidelines are given by the Union. Historically, Brazil had a Commercial Code in 1850 and a Civil Code in 1916, but in 1990 entered into force the "Consumer's Protection Code" and in 2002 a new Civil Code (that revoked both the Civil Code of 1916 and most of the 1850s Commercial Code). The Civil Code of 2002 (Lei nº 10.406/2002) promoted the unification of the civil and commercial obligations, introduce the concept of "enterprise" as substitute of de concept of "tradesman," modified Contract Law, Property Law and, mainly, Tort Law ("Civil Liability"). This Code is the main legal structure of the Private Law System in Brazil. The change is reinforced by the fact that they used, in many circumstances, "open rules:" rules with abstract content, when the judge, case by case, must define the law. In addition, with the other elements (constitutional change, use of principles, judicial activism), the "new" code implies important modifications at the private law scenario.

42. The Civil Code Structure is divided in a General Part and a Special Part. The General Part is very important, as the concepts are an intrinsic need of the civil law, because of its systematic structure, in opposition to the practical and jurisprudential character of common law. The Special Part is divided in Obligations Law (Contracts and Torts), Enterprise Law, Property Law, Family Law, and Inheritance Law.

---

56. See CANOTILHO, MENDES, SARLET, & STRECK (Coord.), Comentários à Constituição do Brasil, 2013, São Paulo, at 45.
57. See COELHO, in CANOTILHO, MENDES, SARLET, and STRECK, Lenio (Coord.), Comentários à Constituição do Brasil, 2013, São Paulo, at 62.

The Civil Code has 2046 articles, the first 232 are in the General Part, and the others are in the Special Part, but the last 49 articles, that are final and transition articles.

43. At the General Part, we can find rules about "persons," "things," "facts (that matters to the Law)," "lawful and unlawful acts," "prescription (statute of limitations)" and "proof." The "Obligation Law" has a "classification," and, then, rules about "transmission," "extinction (including payment)," "nonpayment," "contracts," "unilateral acts," "credit titles" and "civil liability." The "Enterprise Law" defines "Entrepreneur," "corporation," "business unit," register, name, executive board, and other supplementary institutes. The Property Law is, basically, about "possession" and "property/ownership," but there are other rights about assets ("rights in rem"): surface, servitude, usufruct, use, habitation, rights of the promisor buyer of real estate, pledge, mortgage and "antichresis." The Family Law has rules about personal rights (including marriage) and patrimonial rights, including rules about stable union, tutelary and guardianship. Finally, the Inheritance Law disciplines succession in general (legitimate succession, including necessary heirs, testate succession, and asset division).

44. It is fundamental to know that Brazilian Legal System has "microsystems." Besides the main structure (the Civil Code) there are other legal structures, with one or more specific acts ("microsystems"). There is no necessary formal hierarchy between the Civil Code and the acts that consists the microsystems. Legal textbooks refer that is a "source dialogue" between the Civil Code and the acts that consists the microsystems, because there is a reciprocal influence. The main "microsystems," at Private Law, are "Minor Law," "Consumer Law," "Corporate Law," "Capital Market Law" and "Credit Titles Law."

45. The "Consumer Law" (Lei nº 8.078/90) has rules about consumer rights, criminal sanctions (on consumer relations), procedural issues (judicial), and a National System of Consumer's Protection. The "Consumer Rights" consists in "general rules," "consumer national policies," "basic consumer rights," "products and services quality (prevention and liability)," "commercial practices," "contractual protection," "administrative sanctions" (applied by the government agencies), "products and services quality," "health and security protection," "liability by the product/service fact," "liability by the product/service malfunction," "prescription" (statute of limitations), and "disregard of legal entity." The "commercial practices" rules treat about "offer," "publicity," "abusive practices," "debt charge" and "data bank." The "contractual protection" is about "abusive clauses" and "adhesion contracts."

46. The "Corporate Law" is, essentially, composed of the Corporations Law (Lei nº 6.404/76 and Lei nº 10.303/2001), the Judicial Recovery Law (Law nº 11.101/2005), and the One Man Company (Law nº 12.441/2011). Besides the companies (named "*sociedades anônimas*," or SAs), there are other types of partnerships in Brazil's Law System, and the most important are the "Limited Liability Partnerships" (most common legal entities in Brazil) and the "Cooperative Partnerships" (there are important in the agribusiness sector). In the Limited Liability Partnership, there is a partner's limitation of liability. Before they pay-up their share, the liability is limited to the partnership's capital. After they pay-up their share, there is no more any personal liability to the partner. The "Cooperative Partnerships" are regulated by the Law nº 5.754/71 and by the Civil Code. It may not be organized with a view to obtaining profit.

47. Only corporations can use the expression "company" (or the abbreviation Cia.) in the beginning of their names (or use abbreviation S.A. at the end), and only corporations may have their shares traded on stock exchange (if so, the corporation will be regarded as an "open" company; if not, "closed" company). There are three types of shares (ordinary, preference, and "of fruition"). The ordinary share attributes the right of vote. The preference share gives any advantage (priority for receiving dividends, priority in having capital reimbursed, or both of the prior advantages, and there is another advantages possible in the "open" companies). The "fruition share," on the contrary of to distribute dividends, reimburses the shareholder by the share's nominal value. After that, he can buy new shares ("fruition share") that do not increase the company's capital. There are also rules about "administration" ("board of directors," that is mandatory, "audit board," that is mandatory, too, and "advisory board," that is optional, but the "open" companies, when is mandatory). The executive directors are not liable for the company's obligations when the obligation are incurred on behalf of the company "as a consequence of a normal management action." The "Corporations Law" disciplines the changes of corporate status ("transformation," that is the change of type of entity, "incorporation," "merger," named "fusion," and "split," named "schism"). The Judicial Recovery Act is about the Court-controlled procedure where the debtor files voluntary insolvency proceedings aiming to reorganize the company and have it emerge from bankruptcy. It is only for enterprises and "entrepreneurs" (sole traders). The One Man Company Act introduces (2011) in the Brazilian Law System a new institute (named "Empresa Individual de Responsabilidade Limitada" – Individual Enterprise with Limited Liability). The Capital Market Act/ *Lei dos Mercados de Capitais* (nº 4.778/65) is completed by the "CVM Resolutions and Instructions." The CVM ("*Comissão de Valores Mobiliários*") is the "Brazilian SEC – Securities and Exchange Commission." There is only one stock exchange in Brazil ("*São Paulo* Stock Exchange"), that, since 2008, absorbed the Mercantile and Futures Exchange (and now is "BM&FBovespa").

48. The Credit Titles Law is composed by the "Promissory Note and Bill of Exchange Act"/ *Lei das Promissórias e Cartas de Crédito* (Law nº 2.044/1908 and Edict nº 57.663/66 that adopts the Geneva's Uniform Law), the "Check Act"/ *Lei dos Cheques* (nº 7.357/85), the "Duplicate Act"/ *Lei das Duplicatas* (Lei nº 5.474/68), and the "Promissory Note and Bill of Exchange/ Check," that is similar to the law in the USA and Europe. The "duplicate" is a unique credit title that is used in Brazil, especially in credit bank operations. The trader creates a title on the basis of his trades (where there is a term for the payment) and this title is sent to the bank, to anticipate resources. If the consumer does not accept the title (because there is no trade, eventually), the bank demands that the trader substitutes the title, or pay for the loan.

II. Position of the Judiciary

49. Traditionally, in Brazil, like other countries that adopted the "Civil Law" system, Statutory Law is the main (if not the only one) primary authority, giving the judge the role of "*bouche de la loi*" or law's mouth. However, recently, after the Federal Constitution of 1988, the judicial precedent has gained more power. After the Forty-Fifth Amendment, it was included the figure of binding precedents in Brazilian Law System (named "*súmula vinculante*"), as the "New Procedural Civil Code" (Lei nº 13.105/2015) introduced more cases in which the superior courts overpass the judges at first degree, like the "repetitive cases incident resolution" ("*incidente de resolução de demandas repetitivas*," Article 976). These cases reinforce the judicial precedent as primary source of legal authority, giving the Brazilian Judiciary a more influential position.

50. Another fact that contributes to these changes is the idea that the principles are also norms, like the rules, and can be applied by the judges (first degree), and not only of the Supreme Court. It is important to remember that, in Brazil, there are, simultaneously, two models of judicial review about the constitutional rules and principles: the centralized system (by the Supreme Court) and the decentralized system (by any judge or court). Therefore, it's possible to say that, in Brazil, decisions by the courts are formally considered a source of law and there is a mixed system in which the precedent of courts must be followed further decisions.

III. Sources of Private Law in General and of Tort Law in Particular

51. Although, in Brazilian Tort Law, the doctrine differs contractual liability from "extra-contractual" liability, when the Civil Code disposes about "civil liability," it does both for contractual and extra-contractual liability. Therefore, it is impossible to fully separate "contracts" and "torts," because they belong to the same "liability system." Following the tradition of "Civil Law" Systems, in Brazil is used an "integrative" category ("obligation") that works both for contractual and extra-contractual liability. In addition to that, in the Brazilian Law System the "public liability" (the liability imposed to the public agents) has specific principles and rules. There is no civil trial by jury and all "civil liability" cases are decided by a judge or a court ("technical judgment").

§3. Function of the Law of Torts

52. Every tort law system must have a reason to exist, must develop a certain function, given that nothing justifies the fact of incuring costs of transfering a harm for the transfer's sake. In synthesis, a tort law system develops two basic functions, the reparation and the prevention, to which could be added two side functions, punishment and information, concluding, in a holistic manner, that tort law develops the relevant function of maximization welfare.[58]

53. The core function of reparation is developed by tort law, characterized, fundamental, by the obligation to compensate the harm caused, by proportionating to the victims the compensation of the harms suffered. It constitutes the tone of the traditional legal perspective. As highlights Shavell,[59] "the great majority of lawyers, attorneys, judges and, probably, citizens, seems assume that proportionate to victims an equitable compensation for harms is the main function of accidents liability." In fact, throughout the history, the tort law system has been presented as an efficient mechanism of reparation to harm caused to victims. In addition to that, even in current days, through many accident species, tort law still is, if not the only, the best compensation of harms system of all. However, the contemporary society has registered the development of superior mechanisms to secure compensation and make this function developed traditionally by tort law lose its importance. The insurance system, specially, has presented itself as a more effective mechanism in reparation, acting with more celerity and less costs than the tort law system.[60] Moreover, in nowadays, the reparatory function is not an exclusive feature of tort law, being developed jointly or alternatively with other mechanisms in cases of accidents. Therefore, the other functions of civil liability earn a new light.[61]

54. Under the social perspective, it can be inferred that, by making reparation, the harm caused by the accidents does not cease to exist, it only is transferred from the victim to the perpetrator. It does not really return things to a prior state, but only transfers the harm, Schäfer and Ott add that, "the compensatory principle is not enough as a guide" for a civil liability system, being "a mistake to consider the preventive aspect of compensation for harms as a mere welcome side effect. It must be taken in the first place."[62] It must be considered, though, that in the contemporary society, the preventive function does not constitute an exclusive feature of the tort law system. The tort law system is not the only and, possibly not, the most powerful instrument of prevention of accidents. The security matter, *lato sensu*, and public costs are instruments with great power to reduce accidents.[63] It can be verified than in current days, the prevention function of civil liability, by creating incentives to the potential authors and victims for the adoption of conducts that may avoid of

58. See BATTESINI, Direito e Economia, Novos Horizontes no Estudo da Responsabilidade Civil no Brasil, 2011, São Paulo, at 103.
59. See SHAVELL, Foundations of Economic Analysis of Law, 2004, Cambridge, at 267.
60. See PASTOR, Derecho de Daños, 2004, Buenos Aires, at 59.
61. See BATTESINI, Direito e Economia, Novos Horizontes no Estudo da Responsabilidade Civil no Brasil, 2011, São Paulo, at 104.
62. See SCHAEFFER, Hans-Bernd and OTT, Klaus. Economic Analysis of Civil Law, 2004, Cheltenham, at 110.
63. See PASTOR, Derecho de Daños, 2004, Buenos Aires, at 59.

mitigate the costs of accidents, aligns itself as a consistent function for a tort law system.[64]

55. The side function of punishment developed by tort law consists in the imposition to the author, of the monetary additional costs to the effective costs of the harm. In determined situations, to obtain the accidents control in social tolerable levels, it may be justified the imposition of additional deterrent incentives, the punitive damages, whose purpose is to induce a preventive behavior in situations of risk, either by the author of the harmful act, of by persons who find themselves in similar situations, the general deterrence.[65] The punitive function and the compensatory function, in a tort law system, performs its primordial deterrence function considering the socially desirable standards. When the compensatory function is not enough or it is inadequate to create the incentives for prevention, it is performed by the complementation given by the punitive function. It can be inferred, therefore, that, similarly to the sanctions of criminal nature, the punitive function developed by tort law produce the deterrence effect, contributing positively in the control of the accidents risks.[66]

56. As the punitive function, the side function of information is strongly related to the preventive function of a tort law system. According to Schäfer and Ott highlight, as the civil liability is fundamental in the establishment of a determined conduct standard, the rational man standard to act with reasonable care required by social interaction, the norms of tort law must give guidelines for the potential perpetrators for what actions or behaviors are accepted or not.[67] The tort law rules, thus, develop a provisional function, giving information about the less risked manner to act, reducing asymmetries in the information distribution. Using the terminology employed by Joseph Raz, the tort law rules act as a "logarithmic table," as "a map that simplifies the navigation."[68] Therefore, it can be inferred that, as administrative regulation norms, the tort law rules give relevant information about the risks and prevention measures, acting as a referential mark in the behavior shaping of potential authors and victims of accidents.[69]

57. In an elucidative manifestation, Pastor register that the tort law has experimented extraordinary changes in the last forty years, being "its historic function,

---

64. See BATTESINI, Direito e Economia, Novos Horizontes no Estudo da Responsabilidade Civil no Brasil, 2011, São Paulo, at 105.
65. See TESTA, Daños Punitivos, Análisis Económico del Derecho y Teoría de Juegos, 2006, Buenos Aires, at 38–39.
66. See BATTESINI, Direito e Economia, Novos Horizontes no Estudo da Responsabilidade Civil no Brasil, 2011, São Paulo, at 105.
67. See SCHAEFFER, Hans-Bernd and OTT, Klaus, The Economic Analysis of Civil Law, 2004, Cheltenham, at 113.
68. See RAZ, Practical Reasons and Norms, 1999, Oxford, at 60.
69. See BATTESINI, Direito e Economia, Novos Horizontes no Estudo da Responsabilidade Civil no Brasil, 2011 São Paulo, at 106.

constituted fundamentally of proportionate a mechanism of compensation in favor to the victims and deter harmful activities, the first function (compensation) does not be as important as before."[70] Currently, as the author follows, the value of a tort law system must be taking by the results given by the performance of the prevention function and, in situations in which the other mechanisms of compensations cannot act or, by acting, are inferior, in the reparatory function. Therefore, the tort law performs a relevant social welfare function, characterized by "minimizing the costs of accidents, formed by: the probable expected harm; the precaution adopting costs; the costs of supporting the risk, and; the administrative costs of the adopted system." In other words, the social welfare function that is characterized by maximizing the liquid benefit proportioned by the activities involving the risk of accidents, or, the total benefits proportioned to society deducting the social costs of accidents.[71]

58. Considering the current the tort law's scope in Brazil, with the vigency of the 2002's Brazilian Civil Code, in a certain way, it can be affirmed the idea that the civil liability performs a function of promoting the social welfare.[72] In this particular, by disserting about the fundamental principles that oriented the Civil Code of 2002 elaboration, Reale, the coordinator of the commission responsible by the Code's project, highlights the ethnicity, operability and sociability as being the "prevalence of the social upon the individual," as well as, detaching to be "the constant goal of the new Code in the sense to undertake the manifest individualist character of the Civil Code of 1916."[73]

§4. RELATIONSHIP BETWEEN TORT AND CRIMINAL LAW

59. Brazilian legal system distinguishes between tort law and criminal law. Brazilian criminal law is codified in the Criminal Code of 1940 (Decree-Law nº 2.848, of December 7th, 1940), which, in the general part, establishes general rules of application of criminal law, and in the special part, lists all acts that constitutes crimes in Brazil, classifying them in the following categories: crimes against the person, crimes against property, crimes against immaterial property, crimes against organization of labor, crimes against religious feelings, crimes against respect for the dead, crimes against sexual dignity, crimes against the family, crimes against the body's integrity, crimes against peace, faith, and public administration. In addition to the modalities predicted in the Criminal Code, other crimes are predicted in special legislation, namely: bankruptcy crimes (Bankruptcy and Law Judicial Reorganization Law – Law nº 11.101, of February 9th, 2005), crimes against the consumer

70. See PASTOR, Derecho de Daños, 2004, Buenos Aires, at 102.
71. See BATTESINI, Direito e Economia, Novos Horizontes no Estudo da Responsabilidade Civil no Brasil, 2011, São Paulo, at 107.
72. See BATTESINI, Direito e Economia, Novos Horizontes no Estudo da Responsabilidade Civil no Brasil, 2011, São Paulo, at 107–108.
73. See REALE, Visão Geral do Novo Código Civil, 2004, São Paulo, at 12–17.

relations (Consumer's Defense Code – Law nº 8.078, of September 11th, 1990), election-related crimes (Election's Code – Law nº 4.737, of July 15th, 1965), traffic crimes (Brazilian Traffic Code – Law nº 9.503, of September 23rd, 1997), environmental crimes (Law nº 9.605, of February 12th, 1998), among others. In addition to the Criminal Code of 1940 and to special legislation that typifies criminal conducts, the Criminal Procedure Code (Decree-Law nº 3.689, of October 3rd, 1941) provides the rules for criminal enforcement and lawsuits.

60. Criminal Law has as it goal to repress the infractions given as especially reprehensible, and therefore are against the society's interests. While it is part of public law, criminal law is about the sanctions imposed by the State, the main institution responsible for criminal prosecution, which is performed through the Public Ministry. The criminal sanction is measured by the nature of the crime, the gravity of it, the agent's personal characteristics, and other aspects. The criminal sanctions are applied with both the goal to criminalize the inflictor, as it has the goal to prevent new inflictions, by the own inflictor, the "specific prevention" or by other persons, the "general prevention."[74] The tort law, on the other hand, is part of the private law, acting in the ward of specific subjects, which interests were violated by an illicit act performed by a third party. In essence, the tort law constitutes itself in a legal instrument of harms allocation, turning itself to the study of the criteria for selected situations whether the harm caused to third parties should be repaired (and when it should be repaired) and of the criteria for the performance of the repair obligation (how to repair).[75] The main purpose of tort law, as Zweigert and Kötz consigns, consists in specify, among the wide range of everyday events that leads to harm, which ones should be transferred from the victim to the author, according to the justice and fairness ideals that are dominant in society.[76] Even though, it also develops the basic function of prevention and side functions of punishment and information, concisely, the civil liability emphasizes the reparatory function, gravitating the idea of restitution to a situation before the harmful fact.

61. Though a legal fact could generate, at the same time, civil and criminal liabilities, these are independent on their selves. Since they have a different legal nature, the institutes act in distinct realms. In the Brazilian Legal System, the independence of the tort law and criminal law in present in the Article 935 of the Civil Code of 2002. It is, though, a relative independence, thus, many legal norms establish a connection between these systems. The Article 935 itself establishes that it will not be possible "to question about the facts existence, or who is its author, when these questions are decided by criminal courts." Furthermore, in the terms of Article 63 of the Criminal Procedure Code, with the res judicata of the sentence, it is possible to obtain in the civil sphere its execution to ends of harm's reparation.[77]

---

74. See NORONHA, Direito das Obrigações, 2010, São Paulo, at 532–533.
75. See BATTESINI, Tort Law and Economic Development: Strict Liability in Legal Practice, ALACDE, 2015, at 6, available at http://laijle.alacde.org/journal/vol1/iss1/2.
76. See ZWEIGERT & KÖTZ, Introducción al Derecho Comparado, 2002, México, at 660.
77. See DINIZ, Curso de Direito Civil Brasileiro, Responsabilidade Civil, 2009, São Paulo, at 25–26.

§5. Relationship between Contractual and Delictual or Tortious Responsibility

62. The Brazilian Civil Code of 2002 provides a sharp distinction between torts and contracts relations. Contractual relationships are regulated by the Brazilian Civil Code of 2002, in the Title V, Book I – Obligations Law, from the Special Part, in the Articles 421 to 480, and establishes dispositions about contracts in general and in the Title VI, of the same Book, Articles 481 to 853, regulates the diverse species of contracts: buy and sell, exchange, lease contracts, donation, lending, services performance, construction, deposit, mandate, commission, agency, and distribution; real estate management, transportation, insurance, finances, games and gambles, bail, transactions, and compromises. In addition to the modalities predicted by the Civil Code, other contracts are regulated by special legislation, namely: agriculture contracts (Decree nº 59.566, of November 14th, 1966), labor contracts (Labor Law Consolidation – Decree-Law nº 5.452, of May 1st, 1943), and franchising (Law nº 8.955, of December 15th, 1994), among others.

63. Brazilian legal system distinguishes between contractual responsibility and criminal or tortious responsibility. In contractual liability, the reparatory obligation originates itself in the contractual illicit, in the violation of a legal duty predicted in the legal business celebrated between the parties. There is a preexisting legal relation, the contract, which defines the duties that the parties must observe, being the obligation to pay damages originated from the default. In criminal or tortious responsibility, the obligation to repair harms caused are originated by a transgression of a legal duty imposed by law, with the fundament in the respect for persons and things of others, the general duty of *neminem laedere*.[78] In fact, as highlights Cavalieri Filho, the division between contractual and criminal liability is not stable, on the contrary, there is a real symbiosis between these two kinds of liability, since some rules stated by the 2002's Brazilian Civil Code for contractual liability are also applicable in tortious liability.[79]

§6. Protected Interests

64. It is wide the field of interests protected by the Brazilian torts system, with emphasis to the protection of absolute interests, the personality and property rights. The systemic organization of harms susceptible to protection under civil liability is a task traditionally made by the legal theory, being possible to identify some categories of harms namely: personality rights offenses; property rights offenses; offenses to family situations, which generates nurturing rights; offenses to factual situations; and offenses to duties imposed by the general principle of good faith.[80]

78. See NORONHA, Direito das Obrigações, 2010, São Paulo, at 451–453 and 523–525.
79. See CAVALIERI FILHO, Programa de Responsabilidade Civil, 2010, São Paulo, at 15–16.
80. See NORONHA, Direito das Obrigações, 2010, São Paulo, at 465–466.

65. The personality rights, in essence, has by their goal to maintain the respect to life, health, image, name, thought, honor, liberty, and other characteristics of human persons. The general principles applicable to personality rights are object of express prediction in Articles 11 to 21 of the Civil Code of 2002. In addition to that, many dispositions of the Code establish rules of tort law applicable to the violation of personality rights, referring expressively to: homicide, in Article 948; injuries and offenses to health, in Articles 949 and 950; personal injuries, defamations and calumny, in Article 955, and; offenses to the personal liberty, in Article 954.[81]

66. The property rights are the ones, which attributes a direct and immediate power under a thing, which is enforceable to third parties. The property rights are object of express legal prediction in the Book III, Titles II to X, of the Civil Code of 2002, with highlights to the extensive regulation of the property right in Articles 1228–1368. The offenses to property rights assume a special light in the harms caused to mobile and real state property of others, which are widely regulated under the civil liability in Articles 186, 187, 927, 942, and 944 of the Civil Code.[82]

67. Another category of harm that causes civil liability are the offenses to Family situations that generate the obligations of nurturing, such as it is predicted in the Article 948, II, of the Civil Code: "in case of homicide, the damages consist... in the payment of nurturing to persons who the dead owed it, taking in account the probable life span of the victim." In the Brazilian legal system, family law is regulated in the Book IV of the Civil Code of 2002, being the theme of nurturing, predicted in the Articles 1694–1710.[83]

68. Some offenses to factual situations justify protection under the civil liability. It is the case of possession, regulated by the Book III, Title I, of the Civil Code of 2002, which its disturbance or dispossession by third parties authorize the possessor to demand for damages by the harms suffered, in the terms of the Article 1212 of the Civil Code. Another situation that fits in this category is the preservation of nurturing that one of the pair give to the other in situations para-familiar of unions of same-sex persons and cohabitation, according to the Article 1727 of the Civil Code.[84]

69. The legal duty to act according to the good faith in social relations is established by the Brazilian legal system in the Article 422 of the Civil Code of 2002, according to: "the contractors are obliged to ward, either in the conclusion of the contract, as in its execution, the principles of probity and good faith." It is, as highlights Fernando Noronha, the positivation of the general principle of objective good faith, namely: "each person must act, in the social relations according to certain

81. See NORONHA, Direito das Obrigações, São Paulo, 2010, at 466–467, and Nader, Curso de Direito Civil, Responsabilidade Civil, 2014, Rio de Janeiro, at 94–95.
82. See NORONHA, Direito das Obrigações, 2010, São Paulo, at 467.
83. See NORONHA, Direito das Obrigações, São Paulo, 2010, at 467, Nader, Curso de Direito Civil, Responsabilidade Civil, 2014, Rio de Janeiro, at 242–249.
84. See NORONHA, Direito das Obrigações, São Paulo, 2010, at 468–469, and Nader, Curso de Direito Civil, Responsabilidade Civil, 2014, Rio de Janeiro, at 269–275 and 360.

minimum standards of conduct, socially recommended, of loyalty, correction and fairness, which are correspondent to the legitimate expectations of others."[85] Offenses to the duties imposed by the general principle of good faith are qualified as illicit, in the terms of Article 187 of Civil Code of 2002, justifying as such, the application of civil liability either to contractual or extra-contractual illicit, in prior, contemporary or utter moment to the contract's performance.

85. See NORONHA, Direito das Obrigações, 2010, São Paulo, at 470–473.

Part I. Liability for One's Own Acts

Chapter 1. General Principles

§1. Unlawfulness and Fault

70. In Tort Law, a behavior contrary to the law (unlawfulness) is a necessary element (or assumption). There cannot be liability unless the act or fact can be considered unlawful. In inter-personal relations, it is reasonable to suppose that situations in which interests conflict may occur, often provoking interferences that may cause harm to one or both subjects' rights in this relation. However, it is not any relation of this kind that may cause liability, thus many of these are adequate to the legal patterns established by the society. For instance, while in a procurement bid to contract with the public powers, a bidder takes advantage of the other due to a better proposal, that logically cause harm to its defeated concurrent, though, if the procedure is formally regulated it will not generate a compensation obligation to any party. The same rational applies when a driver gets the last spot in a parking lot, preventing the access to the establishment to other drivers, in the same way, there are harms caused to ones who aren't allowed to park, though, since this behavior is not unlawful, it will not make anyone liable for it.

71. As it notes MELLO:[86]

> the act contrary to the law is not sufficient, by itself, to characterize the illicit. In truth, there are situations, that, despite to be, for its nature, contrary to law, for causing a minor harm, are not illicit. Namely, to kill or cause body injuries in self-defense, provoke harm to the wealth of other in necessity state (Civil Code of 2002, Article. 188, I and II; Criminal Code, Article. 23), as damageled fact-acts. In these species, the contrariety to law is not cloaked by illicitly, thus it has other effects than these proper to illicit activities.

72. The notion of illicit can be extracted from the rules inserted in Articles 186 and 187 of the CCB. In Article 186, it can be found the definition of subjective illicitness, which originates from the agent's conduct (fault), which causes harm, even if this damage has no economic content. As for Article 187, it states other grounds for illicitness, which is the abuse of rights. In this case, the illicitness has a strict liability nature, thus independent of the agent's conduct fault verification. However,

86. See MELLO, Teoria do Fato Jurídico – Plano da Existência, 2003, São Paulo, at 219.

it may be civil liability with no illicit activity, thus there is in law an express pre-excluding of illicit (that does not cast out the contrariety to law, or unlawfulness). As there may be illicit activities with no civil liability, thus the act or fact is not imputable to determine agent (§5, and following paragraphs).

§2. Concept of Fault

73. Fault is a voluntary conduct contrary to the duty of care imposed by the law, producing an involuntary harmful event, either foreseen or foreseeable (in narrow sense /*stricto sensu*/, fault or negligent harm) or voluntary (intentional harm). According to Diniz:[87]

> fault in a broad sense is a legal duty's violation, imputable to one, according to intentional fact or omission of due diligence or care, which comprehends: the intent, or intentional harm of a legal duty, the narrow sense liability, characterized by malpractice, imprudence or negligence, without any thoughts on violating a duty... The intent is the conscience will to violate the law, directed to an illicit end, as the fault comprehends the malpractice, imprudence and negligence.

74. As Rodrigues reminds:[88]

> the problem with defining fault is object of debate in foreign literature, where the exact meaning of the word *faute* is under discussion, the expression can be found in the Article 1.382 of the Napoleonic Code, is less ambiguous among us. That is because; regarding to the aquillian liability of Article 186 of the Brazilian Civil Code it defines what is comprehended as a neglect behavior of the harmful act performer agent.

75. The notion of what is "voluntary action or omission, negligence or imprudence" which is quoted in Article 186 was masterly coined by Dias,[89] from Article 159 of the Civil Code of 1916 that had identical content:

> Of fault, characterized ... as negligence or imprudence can be derived other notion that demand a closer look. Thus in this title are, in effect, comprehended the negligence, imprudence and malpractice, which are all related to a nuclear element: the lack of diligence, prevention or care. Negligence is the omission of what is usually done, adjusted the emergent conditions that rules the regular conduct of human business. It is the lack of observance of norms that commands to operate with caution, capacity, solicitude and mindfulness. Consists, the imprudence in the precipitation, unthoughtful, careless and in contradiction to norms of rational procedure. It is the recklessness in act, the

87. See DINIZ, Curso de Direito Civil Brasileiro, 2009, São Paulo, at 41.
88. See RODRIGUES, Direito Civil, vol. 4 – Responsabilidade Civil, 2002, São Paulo, at 146/147.
89. See DIAS, Da Responsabilidade Civil, 2006, Rio de Janeiro, at 135.

malpractice of caution that we must take in our acts. The omission and abstinence are used abusively as synonyms, despite its perceivable difference. Omission is negligence, the act of forget the procedure rules, in developing an activity. Abstinence is inactivity. Generically faces, the omission assumes an initiative. The Abstinence excludes it.
The same occurs with omission and inertia. Both concepts have a negative procedure meaning, though omission has a broader and more complex meaning. In essence, it is fault. However, there are distinctive traces between them.
Negligence relates itself, mainly with dissent; imprudence is connected, more than to other concept, to recklessness; as malpractice, originally to lack of skills.

76. It is always convenient to remind that, in the form determined by the Article 935 of the Civil Code, that the Tort Law is independent of Criminal Law, from which results the standard to determine fault its different in both legal branches. The criteria to define fault in criminal law will always be more accurate than the one required in private law. Therefore, the non-characterization of a conduct as faulty in criminal law will not affect the possibility of the same conduct to be considered as such in Civil Liability.

§3. Duty of Care

77. The duty of care may be related to the agent's omission regarding the activity that, if adopted, may have prevented the harmful event (negligence), or an active behavior of the agent acting hastily, without sufficient consideration of his/her conduct (recklessness imprudence), or furthermore, when the damage is due to technical standards (malpractice or ignorance).

§4. Capacity

78. The notion of illicit would not be complete without a legal system recognize, in addition to unlawfulness, the possibility of the act or fact be bonded to a particular agent, that is called imputability. Direito and Cavalieri Filho,[90] commenting the stated in Article 928 do Código Civil, clarify that:

> As highlighted, there is not liability without harm to a legal duty, which concretized through an illicit act. That implies, firstly, the existence of this duty, and, therefore, the destination to a command to free beings, who can acknowledge it and obey it; secondly, in voluntary practice of a conduct district from the one that is demanded by the law. There is not such violation, as well observes Fernando Pessoa Jorge, when the agent acts deprived of intelligence

90. See DIREITO & CAVALIERI FILHO, Comentários ao Novo Código Civil, 2007, Rio de Janeiro, at 185.

or will. In order to be a violation of a duty, and therefore, an illicit act, is necessary that the agent is in use of his/her mental faculties, in such manner that his/her acts can be morally attributed or imputable, for he/her be the one who caused it. The violation of duty implies in the agent a quality, which is the imputability (Ensaio sobre os Pressupostos da Responsabilidade Civil, Lisboa, 1968, p. 68).
Impute is to attribute to someone the liability for something. Imputability is, thus, the bundle of personal conditions that gives the agent the capacity to respond for the consequences of a conduct contrary to a duty; imputable is the one who could and should have acted in another way.
Of that can be concluded that the imputability is an assumption, not only of fault in a broad sense, as well as liability itself. Therefore, it can be told that there is no way to have liable one for the practice of a harmful act if, in the moment that it had practiced, he/her did not have the capacity to comprehend the reprehensible character of his/her conduct and decide according to this rational.
Two are the elements of imputability: maturity and mental sanity. The first concerns the mental development; the second, its health.
Consequently, imputable if the agent who is mentally sane and developed, who is capable to comprehend the character of his/her conduct and act with this comprehension.

79. During the whole vigency of the Civil Code of 1916, the thought has prevailed that incapables, for being non-imputable, could not be civilly liable. Though the changes introduced by the Civil Code of 2002, in the highlighted Article 928, has permitted the incapable's liability (mentally disabled and/or under age of 18 years), through a mitigation and subsidiarity criteria. The incapable will respond for the harms caused by him/her who cause to people if the people for him responsible have no obligation to do it or does not have enough means to repair it. The generic inimputability it, here, void in privilege to an exceptional norm that predicts the notion of the victim compensation, that contradicts the protective rule of the incapable.

80. According to Diniz,[91] "the imputability, element that constitutes the fault, it due to personal conditions (conscience and will) of one who practiced the harmful act, in a fashion that consists in the possibility to do something as someone's act as proceeding by a free will." The author recognizes as "exceptions to the imputability" the situations of the underage and demented persons (incapable), in the case of the Article 928, thus, even with imputability there is civil liability.

91. See DINIZ, Curso de Direito Civil Brasileiro, 2009, São Paulo, at 45.

Chapter 2. Specific Cases of Liability

§1. Liability of Professionals

81. In the case of professional activities, it must be firstly established the distinction between the liabilities emerged from the contractual obligations breaches (which are not this study's subject) and those resulting from absolute duties violation (or Civil Liability in *stricto sensu*). Any service performed by a professional will create contractual obligations, despite the fact of being a mutually beneficent contract. However, we will examine only the civil liability, which has its origins in an act (licit or illicit) that is not framed as negotiable in its nature (obligation breaches that would be translated, thus, into relative illicit). Siding with the criminal liability, the administrative liability (agencies and syndicate controls of the professional performance), and distinguished from the contractual liability is located the Civil Liability (*stricto sensu*) of professionals in a specific environment. Which its regulation origins essentially in rules and principles found in the Brazilian Civil Code, along with situations under the domain of the Consumer's Protection Code (Law nº 8.078/90).

I. In General: Standard of Care for "Experts"

82. The Brazilian Civil Code (Article 186), differently from the Criminal Code (Article 18, II), does not include malpractice as a form of fault. Though, as highlights Theodoro Junior,[92] "that does not mean that malpractice is not a form of fault to configure a civil liability," not being its situation distinctive from negligence and recklessness. What really defines malpractice in particular, is the exigence, regarding the imputable agent, of a technical, specific, knowledge, which is not required in the other cases of negligence and recklessness.

83. Being the notion more common among the doctrine, "it is configured the malpractice when the harm origins itself in the inobservance of technical norms,"[93] or, as states Coelho,[94] "it is the non-intentional fault in the profession or job performance," wherefrom its relevance is locates where the professional liability is examined.

84. The standards to define malpractice can vary from case to case, and depend fundamentally from technical criteria, which its rule making is mainly made from control agencies to profession exercise (for instance, the Medicine National

92. THEODORO JUNIOR, Comentários ao Novo Código Civil, 2003, Rio de Janeiro, at 106.
93. See NADER, "Curso de Direito Civil, vol. 7 – Responsabilidade Civil," 2014, Rio de Janeiro, at 92.
94. See COELHO, Curso de Direito Civil, vol. 2, 2005, São Paulo, at 309.

Council,[95] the Brazilian BAR Association – OAB,[96] the Federal Council of Engineer and Agronomy and the Urbanism,[97] and Architecture Council of Brazil[98]).

II. Medical Practitioners

85. A sensible matter, the Medical Practitioner's Liability is considered, according to Borges, as part of the general system of liability, though, its legal binding to the Consumer Law's system, as the author states,[99] the medical civil liability obeys the same principles of the general tort law, according to which one who perform determined act or intention, or even with "simple fault," cause harm, have to repair it. It is demanded for its configuration the fault, or, to show that there was not compliance to essential legal duties that originates from the medical services performance, which characterizes fault, in any of its shades (negligence, malpractice, and recklessness), or intent in fulfilling its obligations. As the author lectures further,[100] can be drawn the idea that "the extra-contractual liability is configured due the facts that binds face to face the medic and the patient, having the prior the duty to do medical assistance, for instance, an emergency … ."

86. The main consequence of this distinction lies in the field of the burden of proof's distribution, thus in the contractual medical liability will be bonded to consumer law, in which, despite the rule contained in §4° of Article 14 of Law n° 8.078/90. It is common the inversion of the burden of proof, based upon VIII of Article 6, of the same law. This distinction, though, was mitigated with the emergency of the new Brazilian Procedure Code. In its Article 373, §1, the code predicts the possibility (in the cases predicted by law or facing the peculiarities of causation related to the impossibility or exclusive difficulty of achieving the goal... or better conditions to achieve proofs of the contrary fact) of the judge to redistribute the burden of proof, "if it makes through fundamental decision." Diniz[101] gives as examples the fake medical certificate that supply consent – it could deter what constitutes a liability for omission – of a person who is not habilitated to practice medicine, to not order the immediate removal of a wounded person in emergency situations and others.

95. CONSELHO FEDERAL DE MEDICINA. Código de Ética Médica. Available at http://portal.cfm.org.br.
96. ORDEM DOS ADVOGADOS DO BRASIL, Estatuto da OAB. Available at http://www.oab.org.br.
97. CONSELHO FEDERAL DOS ENGENHEIROS E AGRONOMIA. Código de Ética Profissional. Available at http://www.confea.org.br.
98. CONSELHO DOS ARQUITETOS E URBANISTAS DO BRASIL. Código de Ética e Disciplina dos Arquitetos e Urbanistas. Available at http://www.caubr.gov.br.
99. See BORGES, Erro Médico nas Cirurgias Plásticas, 2014, São Paulo, at 211.
100. *Ibid.* Where if said that "the personal liability of the liberal professionals will be verified only through analysis of fault," at 214.
101. See DINIZ, Curso de Direito Civil Brasileiro, vol. 7 – Responsabilidade Civil, 2009, São Paulo, at 296.

III. Legal Practitioners

87. In the case of attorneys, the civil liability is also, mainly of contractual nature, but there are situations where the professional can be charged by violations of an absolute duty, even if lacking a business bond. This hypothesis, for instance, of offense, in the exercise of profession against other professional, a judge or justice official, where the relationship of representation of a client is absent.

IV. Builders and Architects

88. In Brazil, the Civil Liability is generically ruled by Article 927 of the Brazilian Civil Code, though; the called "Consumption Relations" are predicted in the Consumer's Defense Code. Are considered as "consumption" relations, these celebrated between consumers and suppliers, being the firsts, according to the CDC, "Art. 2° Consumer is every physical or legal person who acquires or use product or services as a final destination," as well as a plurality of persons that may be in these relations, as the paragraph of the same article states, "the collective of persons, even if indeterminable, that have intervene in consumption relations;" and are suppliers, according to the Article 3, "Art. 3° Supplier is any physical or legal person, public or private, national or foreigner, as the depersoned entities that develop production, assembling, creation, construction, transformation, import, export, distribute or commercialize products or services." As it can be observed, the activities of creation and construction, destines to a physical or legal person as final destination, and configures, according to Brazilian Law, a consumption relation.

89. Therefore, the Builders and Architects liability are under the jurisdiction of the Consumer's Defense Code, and not by the general predictions of the Brazilian Civil Code of 2002, by the criteria of the specificity of the applicable Law, according to the criteria of the current jurisprudence.[102] The substantial distinction between the builder and architect's liability, can be found in different kinds of factual relations, where: there is a builder company and a liberal professional architect, where: The architect is hired to do the Project and to be held liable by the execution of the project; both builders and architect were hired separately by the consumer.

90. According to the current jurisprudence, the Architect's liability is predicted in the Article 14 §4 of the Consumer's Defense Code, considered a "liberal professional's liability" case, where "The personal liability of liberal professionals will be configured through the verification of fault," while the builder's liability is predicted by the article's caput, there "Article 14. The supplier of services responds, independently of fault, by the reparation of the harms caused to the consumers by defect in the services performance, as for the insufficient information about its fruition and risks." Therefore, the first distinction that can be made about the Architects and Builder's liabilities, throughout the Article 14 of the CDC's reading is that the

102. TJRS. AC, N° 70016450728. Nona Câmara Cível. Comarca de Porto Alegre. Des.ª Iris Helena Medeiros Nogueira. 08/12/2006. Porto Alegre.

first is liable through the institute of Negligence, as the second group is liable through Strict Liability, through the risks created, not being necessary the proof of fault, but only of causation and the harm itself for the generation of the compensatory damages payment's obligation to rise.

91. In addition, in the case of hiring of the liberal professional for the building company, the architect's liability is joined with the builder regarding the project and its execution defects;[103] as if the Architect contract the building team, he/she will be liable for all details originated by his supervision duties and conformities to the project. And, finally, in the case of separated contracted architects and builders, the architect's liability will be restricted to the Project defects as the builders will respond to the defects regarding unconformities to the Project created.[104]

92. As for the burden of proof, Cavalieri Filho states that, "As highlighted before, the liberal professionals, as services performers that they are, are not out of the discipline of the Consumer's Defense Code. The only exception that was made for them is about the strict liability. And it was necessary to do so, thus they are subject to the other principles of consumer's defense code – information, transparency, good-faith and burden of proof reversal etc.,"[105] this way, it is responsibility to the liberal professional to proof that there are none unconformities with the Project that provoked the harm or that the Project itself is not defective under the available techniques; as the builder must do the same by its turn, due the predicted in Article 6°, VIII, where "Art. 6° are basic rights of the consumer: VIII – the ameliorant of the defense of his/her rights, including the burden of proof's inversion to his behalf, in the civil procedure, when, to the judge's rational, its verisimilar the plea or when hypo sufficient, following the ordinary rules of experience."

§2. Liability of Public Authorities (Governmental Liability)

93. Under Brazilian Law, public authorities and the private persons providing public service are civilly liable for harms caused by an third party acting as their official representative, even while exercising public sovereign immunity. This widely accepted principle is currently undisputed and it is an object of constitutional provision. In the terms of Article 37, §6th, of the Federal Constitution, "the legal persons of public law, and private law performing public services will be liable by the harms caused by their agents, in this quality to third parties, secured the redress right against the responsible in cases of intent or fault." An analogue disposition can be found in the Article 43 of the Civil Code of 2002: "the legal persons

103. TJRS. AC, N° 70018927665. Nona Câmara Cível. Comarca de Rio Grande. Des.ª Marilene Bonzanini Bernardi. 26/12/2007. Porto Alegre.
104. TJRS. RI, N° 71001305770. Primeira Turma Recursal Cível. Comarca de Guaíba. Dr. Ricardo Torres Hermann. 04/10/2007. Porto Alegre.
105. See CAVALIERI FILHO, Programa de Responsabilidade Civil, 2010, São Paulo.

of internal public law are civilly liable by the acts of their agents in this quality that cause harm to third parties, reserved the redress right against the harm's causers, it by them there is fault or intent."

94. As it can be inferred from the Article 37, §6th, of the Federal Constitution, for the Public Power respond civilly by an act performed in the realm of Public Administration, a few requisites must be fulfilled. It is necessary the occurrence of a harm, not being enough the illicit of the administrative act for one to demand the compensation. The harmful conduct must be attributed to the officer or agent of the legal person of public law or private law performing public services. The agent, in practicing the act, must do it while exercising the public function and not while in his/her private life. It must be a causation nexus between the harmful conduct and the verified harm. Moreover, the administrative act must be illicit.[106]

95. Regarding the illicit nature of the act, the imputation nexus, the prevalent theory in Brazilian law distinguishes between comissive and omissive conducts. Regarding the comissive conducts, it is a consensus that the State's liability is objective (strict liability), funded in the theory of administrative risk by the Article 37, §6th of the Federal Constitution. As for the omissive conducts, doctrine[107] and jurisprudence diverge between the adoption of strict liability[108] and the negligence system, funded in the theory of *faute du service.*[109]

96. Regarding the State's liability, are applicable: the exemption clauses of self-defense, regular exercise of a right and deterioration or destruction of other's things or harm to a person in order to remove imminent harms (Article 188 of the Civil Code of 2002); the causation exemption clauses, the fortuity, act of god and exclusive victim's fault (doctrinaire and jurisprudential construction); as is admitted the reduction of the damage's value by the contributory fault of the victim (Article 945 of the Civil Code). In addition to the fact that, when admitted the negligence as fundament, are not applicable the liability of the State in cases in which the public office or agent acts without intent or fault *stricto sensu.*[110]

97. It is wide the spectrum of application of State's Civil Liability, comprehending the administrative acts practiced by the three power spheres, the Legislative, the Judiciary and mainly, the Executive, thereby are frequent the legal demands funded

---

106. See NADER, Curso de Direito Civil, Responsabilidade Civil, 2014, Rio de Janeiro, at 319–320, and RODRIGUES JUNIOR, MAMEDE and ROCHA, Responsabilidade Civil Contemporânea, 2011, São Paulo, at 403–409.
107. See CAVALIERI FILHO, Programa de Responsabilidade Civil, 2010, São Paulo, at 246–247 and 251–255, and SEVERO, Tratado da Responsabilidade Pública, 2009, São Paulo, at 166–168.
108. STF, 2ª Turma, RE 180.602-8/SP, Relator Ministro Marco Aurélio, DJ 16.04.1999, at 1018. Brasília.
109. STF, 1ª Turma, RE 170.014-9/SP, Relator Ministro Ilmar Galvão, DJ 13.02.1998, at 633. Brasília.
110. See NADER, Curso de Direito Civil, Responsabilidade Civil, 2014, Rio de Janeiro, at 331–332, and RODRIGUES JUNIOR, MAMEDE and ROCHA, Responsabilidade Civil Contemporânea, 2011, São Paulo, at 410-412.

by the omission of the State in the performance of public services in fields such as health, public security, infra-structure and transportation.[111]

§3. Abuse of Rights (Civil Rights)

98. Along with the subjective illicit described in Article 186, the Civil Code defines a situation of strict liability when the holder of a right exercises it in an abusive manner, exceeding the limits imposed by their economic or social purpose of its activity, by good faith or social costumes (Article 187). As Nader says:[112]

> according to the Article 187 of the Civil Code, innovative in legislative terms which has it source in the Article 334 of the Portuguese Civil Code, practices an illicit one, that exercises its right, not respecting the limits given by its economic or social purposes, by good faith or by social costumes. With the breach of either one of these rules, emerges the legal figure of the abuse of rights, which subjects the agent to civil liability. The illicit act may characterize when the agent, in exercising his right aims to cause harm to other, constituting these, this as the great aim of its conduct.

Furthermore,[113] it emerges from the content of the 37th statement of the 1st Private Law Journey (*I Jornada de Direito Civil*), promoted by the Federal Justice Council (Conselho da Justiça Federal), "therefore, it can be interpreted that the abuse of rights is prior to the element of fault: the civil liability based on abuse of rights is independent to fault and is based only in the end-goal criteria."

99. In monographic work about the subject Miragem[114] clarifies the difficulties of the reconstruction and conception of a new theory of abuse of rights in Brazil through the Article 187 of the Civil Code:

> An apparent difficulty in surpass these questions takes many scholars, including the ones that have dedicated themselves to the subject recently, to avoid implicitly and explicitly the bound to the Article 187 of the Civil Code the theory of the abuse of rights. In this sense, for instance, the prominent Professor Judith Martins-Costa states that,"in identifying the mentioned article of the Code as the basis to the prohibition of a contradictor behavior (*venire contra factum proprium*), it is examined it under the characterization of inadmissible exercise of legal positions in legal rational exposed initially by Menezes Cordeiro, regarding the Portuguese Law." She justifies her rational, thus,

111. See SEVERO, Tratado da Responsabilidade Pública, 2009, São Paulo, at 288 et seq. and STOCO, Tratado de Responsabilidade Civil, 2014, São Paulo, at 1364 et seq.
112. See NADER, Curso de Direito Civil – Responsabilidade Civil, 2014, Rio de Janeiro, at 120.
113. *Ibid.*, at 124.
114. See MIRAGEM, Abuso do Direito = Proteção da Confiança e Limite ao Exercício das Prerrogativas Jurídicas no Direito Privado, 2009, Rio de Janeiro, at 122 and following.

considering that "the main distinction between the abuse of rights and the inadmissible exercise of legal position, it, therefore, in the fact that the last does not imply fault as element of the factual support to the rule." It can be inferred from the author's preoccupation in dethatch the relation to the Article 187's rules the exigence of a voluntary or faulty behavior, and thus, deriving her rejection to qualify it as an abuse of rights.

It can be inferred, though, that the conception of the abuse, exclusively through its subjective element, it's nothing else than the recognition of the absolute identity between the abusive act and the emulation, which restricts its reach to the same limits to the liability for fault, which contradicts the tendencies of the contemporary law and even the considerations that are defended and qualified by the doctrine of today.

The jurisprudence, at first, have opted by the subjective conception of the abuse, either by its simplicity or by a special care to the law's intensity, though, as it denoted the exclusive intention of the agent to cause harm to other, what would pose itself in contradiction to the elementary social principle of solidarity. Furthermore, it can be inferred that the conception of the abuse of right through its subjective angle, cannot find more relevance in the doctrine, except for recent exceptions.

The main question, though, seems to lie in the possibility to conceive a hypothesis of strict liability, without exigence of fault as is the case of the Article 187 of the Civil Code, and – respected the mentioned examined distinctions – it can be perceived a wide use of the concept of abuse and abusive behavior in other laws, as occurs in the notorious case of the Consumer's Defense Code.

100. As seen, the Abuse of Rights is a controversial concept by its effect on the doctrine of strict liability and extension of the illicit act. Furthermore, Miragem[115] continues his lecture on the legal nature of the abuse of rights, and its repercussions on this extension of the concept of illicit as opposed to the institute of fault:

> ... In the current private law, thus, illicit and fault are not the same. The notion of civil torts, which were inherited from the classic private law, gives space to a double possibility of illicit, which abandons the ancient concentration in the notion of fault e and starts to concentrate in the violation of a legal duty. Thus, the perfect frame of strict liability, without fault, as a second general clause of illicit in the Civil Code of 2002. This substantial alteration is part of a movement of functionalization of the Brazilian private law, which objectives and goals of legal institutes such as predicted in legislation are now preferred in relation to the will and fault, that can be perceived easily in the grounds of the social function of many institutes such as property, contracts and firms.
>
> This is as well the rational coined in the Private Law Journey (*Jornadas de Direito Civil*), promoted by the Superior Court of Justice (Superior Tribunal de Justiça) under the coordination of Minister Ruy Rosado Aguiar Júnior, who has reunited private lawyers from the whole country to examine the Civil Code,

115. See MIRAGEM, Abuso do Direito = Proteção da Confiança e Limite ao Exercício das Prerrogativas Jurídicas no Direito Privado, 2009, Rio de Janeiro, at 122 and following.

and has approved among its statements to the interpretation and application of the law, the 37th statement with the following content: "Art. 187. The civil liability from the abuse of rights does not depend of fault and has its fundament only in the criteria objective-finalistic." Which means that, it is recognized the abuse as fundament of strict liability, and, as a reflex the possibility of an objective illicit, with no fault, as established in the second general clause of illicit in the new Civil Code.

Contradicting what it could be supposed, the exigence of a current comprehension of the abuse of rights, that casts out the intent and fault as assumptions for its characterization, it is not enough for the frame of the abuse of rights as an adequate solution to a series of situations in which the exercise of legal powers and subjective rights opposes to social acceptable behaviors. In a broad sense, an apparent case of abuse of rights, such as an independent category or as an illicit in the general Private Law's theory, it should be attributed to it two factors: (a) its wrongful recognition as a subjective liability, that require intent or fault; (b) de great development of the strict good faith as source of legal duties. Regarding the first factor examined in details. In regard to the strict good faith and its various implications to the contemporary Brazilian Private Law, though, is what is needed to establish as a comparative effort to the abuse of rights, in order to identity its utility or not.

The development of the strict good faith as a source of annex or side legal duties in Brazilian law is attributed in a great measure to the studies of Clóvis do Couto e Silva and his well-known work The Obligation as a Process. This work, notably inspired by German Law, the Gaucho master has defined good Faith, regarding the obligation's law as, "objective maximum that determines the raise of duties beyond those that the convention explicitly constitutes. In the same time, the good faith in strict identities the presence, in obligation's law, and on the side of the main duties of performance, the secondary duties and the annex duties, oriented directly to the fulfillment of the performance (secondary) or to fulfill the contractual end and the protection of the wealth of the parties (annex).

101. Regarding the application of the abuse of rights is characterized as a repercussion of the good faith principle, combined with figures of exemption clauses that will be further addressed in this work:[116]

As for its application, with great utility for the evolution of the Brazilian Law, the good Faith has occupied the role, in terms of legal principal, mainly in the obligations law field. This situation, even that it didn't eclipsed entirely a second prestigious figure, that is definitely more related to real state rights as the social function or social, has made the good faith to develop with great vitality among the Brazilian doctrine and jurisprudence in the last two decades.

In this context, the renaissance of the abuse of rights, through the Article 187 of the Civil Code, can be questioned for its contemporaneity and utility due,

116. See MIRAGEM, Abuso do Direito = Proteção da Confiança e Limite ao Exercício das Prerrogativas Jurídicas no Direito Privado, 2009, Rio de Janeiro, at 122 and following.

mainly the great role of the good Faith in the legal system prior to the Civil Code as in its own as it can be observed in Articles 113, 77, 128 and 422.
As referred before, among the well-known critiques to the abuse of rights, Menezes Cordeiro has said that it cannot be seen as a factor of rupture with the legal continuity brought by the Napoleonic codification and the further doctrine. In this sense, he makes a cult argumentation to demonstrate what he comprehends as the decay of the abuse of rights, rather indicating and interpreting the Article 334 of the Portuguese Civil Code, based on the good faith perspective as the inadmissible exercise of legal positions. 82 Currently, the Portuguese master is revisiting in part these positions, identifying the merits in the abuse of rights theory, specially as an instrument of stability and correction of the legal system.
In German law, the good Faith fulfill this kind of corrective function of bad exercise of liberty, maybe for the same fact that the §226 of the German Civil Code (BGB), in which its identified the abuse of rights figure and it has established it in order to condemn an emulative act (" the exercise of a rights is inadmissible if it has for its end to cause harm to other"), in the same way as the § 826 of the BGB ("One who, in a way that attempts against the good costumes, inflicts with intent harm to other its obliged to pay damages for the harm caused"). According to Menezes Cordeiro, the §826 had two problems, since the intent's assumption let "without cover a series of negligent activities or simply, unprovable." Even though, the more problematic would be, "the obligation to pay damages would deter the most adequate remedy for the inadmissible act; the cessation of the abuse itself."
It seems, though, that the simple denial of the abuse of rights in the interpretation of the Article 187 of the Brazilian Civil Code (or Article 334 of the Portuguese Civil Code), does not add elements to refine the mentioned goal of the statement, which is precisely the exercise of a subjective right in an anti-social fashion. Consolidated as is, the question about the violator conduct's nature in the established limits of the rule about the owner of the right's conduct, it can be noted that, among the good Faith, two new concepts are incorporated, which the doctrine and jurisprudence have little or none attention, either before or after the new legislation.
As mentioned prior, while regarding the good Faith it can be observed a species of effervescence in our doctrine and jurisprudence, the same cannot be told of the other two limits expressed by the rule, the economic or social goal and the costumes. This has a greater relevance while it can be perceived that, while it is wide the matters for which it can be applied, the strict good faith has an application profile fairly focused in the obligational relation, either between private parties or between private parties and the state.

102. Furthermore, Miragem address the social or economic function and good costumes open concepts relations to the abuse of rights application, where:[117]

117. See MIRAGEM, Abuso do Direito = Proteção da Confiança e Limite ao Exercício das Prerrogativas Jurídicas no Direito Privado. Forense, 2009, Rio de Janeiro, at 122 and following.

Concerning the subjective right's economic or social goal, it is true that the great debate about the theme is framed by the property rights, as for the social function of ownership, mainly after the Constitution of 1988, therefore, are barely developed the social function of contracts and firms in the New Civil Code. Though, it can be forgotten that as it is established by the Article 187, are not a few, but all subjective rights are, according to the legislation, aiming to some economic or social goals, and therefore, must be examined through this perspective to evaluate its exercise by its owner's activity conformity. The same can be told about the good costumes, which an historic bound in our jurisprudence to sexual morality or a standard lifestyle, has deterred the great possibilities of the concept to limit the will power in the exercise of the subjective liberty and an anti-social and contrary to social interest behavior. Therefore, it seems clear the importance of Article 187, thus it embodies a renewed conception of the abuse of rights, bounded to the fulfillment of legal goals external to the Code, as the influence and application of constitutional rules to legal relations of Private Law. Which means that, in the evaluation of non-compliance between the exercise of legal situation and the values assured by the legal-constitutional system." In this case, the important virtue of the rediscovery of the abuse of rights and its utility as a safeguard to the consequences of the strict application of the law. As it was conceived, the concept of the abuse of rights can establish a bound to be incorporated by the Private Law rules, in the grounds of civil liability and in the other grounds of personal protection – as for instance, regarding the validity or inefficacy of acts and legal business in general – the constitutional rules regarding private relations. As for example, the constitutional rules regarding personality rights, contract law, property rights and family law.

§4. Injury to Reputation and Privacy

103. There is no specific legislation in Brazil, which guarantee is the civil liability in case of violation of human rights that may cause harms. Therefore, the normative fundamentals (generic) comes through the Civil Code.

104. There is a constitutional prediction (Article 5º, X) for cases of damages for intimacy violation, private life, honor, and person's images, all cases of manifestation of personality rights. This constitutional warranty is evidenced by the presence of the specific chapter in Title I (of Natural Persons), of Book I (of Persons), of the General Part of the Civil Code, entitled "Of the Personality Rights." In this chapter, more precisely, in Article 12, the rule establishes the possibility of the use of inhibitory remedies (menace or injury cessation) for the protection of personality rights, which does not casts "barriers to other sanctions predicted by law." In the civil bench, it is contemplated the liability of damages to harms caused, including the extra-patrimonial ones, in the same terms of the generic prediction defined by the Article 927 of the Code.

§5. Interference with Contractual Relations

105. As mentioned before, in Brazilian law, mainly, is not clear the line between the contractual liability and the extra-contractual liability, the fact is even more perceivable in the case of professional's liabilities. The distinction mitigation, from the practical point of view is also result of the similarities that can be verifies in other legal systems from the "continental model" (Civil Law), in Brazil, it is recognized the unity of the obligations concept (either it having contractual or extra-contractual origins), letting this debate to be restricted to the theoretical plane.[118] Some relevance may emerge from certain effects, such as the initial term to delay interests (if the liability is contractual, the interests are counted from the warrant of the defendant; if extra-contractual, it is counted from the illicit act performance, according to the Articles 397 and 398 of the Civil Code). There is a decision from the Superior Court of Justice (Superior Tribunal de Justiça)[119] that recognizes as contractual the civil liability from preliminary negotiations breaches, but the matter is controversial,[120] as the very decisions acknowledges.

106. Therefore, there are cases, in professional's liability, with the recognition of a precontractual liability (and, without contract, extra-contractual), due the violation of derived duties from the good faith (indication and clarification, help and cooperation). This possibility is more evident when it is dealt with a consumption relationship, thus, in the terms of Law n° 8.078/90 (Consumer's Defense Code – CDC), these hypothesis, the publicity (done by services and products suppliers) has an offer nature (Article 30), being source of liability, despite of the formation of a contract.[121] However, there may be an application of the strict good faith principle also in situations not configured as with analogical fundaments, observing that the same principle can be founded in the 2002's Brazilian Civil Code.[122]

---

118. In the special appeal (STJ, Recurso Especial 1367955/SP), judged in 18/03/14, the Relator, Ministro PAULO SANSEVERINO, highlighted that there are none ontological differences between the contractual and extra-contractual liabilities.
119. In the same Special Appeal (REsp 1367955/SP), is stated that by legislative option, the civil liability originated from negotiation breaches has contractual nature.
120. About the topic, "preliminary negotiations and their effects," See LÔBO Direito Civil – Contratos, 2011, São Paulo: "the discussion about if the liability is contractual or extra-contractual or mixed is given until nowadays. In the contractual relation it is biased to the extra-contractual liability according to the general rules of harms. In the consumption relations, there is a bias in the specialized doctrine for extra-contractual liability in strict nature," at 86.
121. STJ, Recursos Especiais 1199117/SP, de 18/12/12; 1261513/SP, de 27/08/13; 1344967/SP, de 26/08/14 e 1428801/RJ, de 27/10/15. Brasília.
122. In the already summoned Special Appeal (Recurso Especial 1367955/SP), the Relator highlighted that the principle of strict good faith is given since the formation of the obligations bound, before even the celebration of the legal business intended by the parts. In fact, before the conclusion of the legal business, are established between the persons' certain factual relationships, called "social contacts," from which derives legal duties, which their violations imply civil liability.

Part II. Liability for Acts of Others

107. The main rule in Torts is that one responds for its own acts. It is what is traditionally called direct liability, simple liability, or simply liability for one's own acts, as seen in part I of this study. In some hypothesis, though, a person might be indirectly liable: either for harms caused by others, also known as third parties liability, vicarious liability or simply liability for acts of others in *stricto sensu*; either for harm caused by inanimate things which is also known as fact of things, or even by the guard of inanimate things or simply liability for things; or by harms caused by animals, which is conventionally called animal fact liability, guard of animal liability, or simply liability for animals.[123] As the indirect liability or complex liability represents an exception to the main principle, casting a liability for one that didn't act directly for the harm concretion, it is necessary a legal qualified element, which is related to a duty of guard, vigilance, or custody between this person and the person directly liable for the harm, or to the thing or animal which caused the direct harm causation.[124]

123. See NORONHA, Direito das Obrigações, 2010, São Paulo, at 514–515, and DINIZ, Curso de Direito Civil Brasileiro, Responsabilidade Civil, 2010, São Paulo, at 528–529.
124. See CAVALIERI FILHO, Programa de Responsabilidade Civil, 2012, São Paulo, at 191 and 212.

Chapter 1. Vicarious Liability

108. In vicarious liability or liability for acts of others in *stricto sensu*, as highlights the main Brazilian author in Torts, José de Aguiar Dias,[125] the liability's fundament is "in the fact of that certain people have the duty to survey the procedure of others, whose inexperience or malice can cause harm to third parties," it lies in "the duty of surveillance imputable too one that declares himself liable." It configures, thus, a complex relation, with the existence of two passive subjects, liable upon the victim rights and therefore entitled to pay damages: by one hand, the agent who practiced the harmful act to other's right, the "de facto author" of the harm; on the other hand, the agent liable by equity and for the acts made by the de facto agent. In fact, the act practiced by the de facto author configures an immediate causation, being the violation of the duty of surveillance legally established to specific people the mediate causation, thus the legal fundament of the liability for acts of others.[126]

109. In Brazil, during the rule of the now revoked Civil Code of 1916, there was an intense scholar and jurisprudential debate about the nature of the legally liable agent by the de facto agent's acts position in relation to the victim regarding if it should be considered subjective emerging from the notion of the presumption of guilt/negligence or if it should be considered subject of strict liability based on the risk theory. The promulgation of the New Civil Code of 2002 has ended the controversy, establishing in its Articles 932 and 933 the strict liability in the described cases.[127] However, the code brings here the concept of strict secondary liability, since that is necessary the concurrency of two liability's systems: the legally liable agent, which is strict liability, and the liability of the de facto agent given by his/her negligence. Both, however, are jointly liable towards the victim, in accordance with Article 942, sole paragraph of the Civil Code of 2002.[128]

110. In the Brazilian Torts current system,[129] there are many hypothesis of vicarious liability or liability for acts of others in *stricto sensu*, which are regulated under the Articles 932 and 933 of the Civil Code of 2002: the strict liability of parents for the damages caused by their underage children, predicted by Article 932, I; the strict liability of the tutor and curator by damages caused by their pupils and curate's, predicted by Article 932, II; the strict liability of employers for the harm caused by employees, servants and agents, predicted by Article 932, III; the strict liability of hotel, bed and breakfast, houses or establishment where one can find shelter for money owners for the harm caused by their guests, tenants and students, predicted by Article 932, IV; and the strict liability of one who freely has participated of product of crime until the quantity he/her is liable for the damages caused by the criminals, predicted in Article 932, V. Furthermore, the Articles 1.175 and 1.178 of the Civil Code establish the firm's liability for their branches' acts.

125. See DIAS, Da Responsabilidade Civil, 2006, Rio de Janeiro, at 742–743.
126. See LIMA, A responsabilidade civil pelo fato de outrem, 1972, Rio de Janeiro, at 20.
127. See PEREIRA, Responsabilidade Civil, 2012, Rio de Janeiro, at 122–124.
128. See CAVALIERI FILHO, Programa de Responsabilidade Civil, 2012, São Paulo, at 193–194.
129. See Part III. Forms of Strict Liability, Ch. 5. Others.

§1. EMPLOYEE/EMPLOYER

111. In Article 932, III, combined with Article 933, both from the Civil Code of 2002, is predicted the strict liability of the employer for the harm caused by their employees or servants, in the exercise of their jobs or by their jobs. Either are based on the substitution theory, in which the employer, by ordering the services of the employee its taking advantage of an instrument to let him exercise multiple firm tasks, extending his own activity, or based in the profit risk, in which the employer benefits from the results of the activity developed by its employee, and therefore assuming the risks from it, the employer's strict liability from the harm caused by their employees presupposes the existence of a legal contractual bind from which results the duty of the employer to secure the employee's or one that provides him services activities for third parties.[130]

112. In the concretion of the command contained in Article 932, III, of the Civil Code, are revealed the important concepts of employer and employee which are expressly announced by the Labor Law Consolidation (CLT) (1).[131] It is considered employer "the individual or collective firm, which, assuming the risks of the economic activity, admits, give wage and directs the personal performance of services," considered equal to employers for effects of job relations the "liberal professionals, the charity, the dominical associations or not-for profit institutions which may admit workers as employees" (Article 2, caput and paragraph first, of the Labor Law Consolidation). It is considered employee "any person who perform services of non-eventual nature to the employer, under dependence of him and through wage in return" (Article 3 of the Labor Law Consolidation).

113. It is fundamental for the application of Article 932, III, of the Civil Code, the existence of a dependence relation or subordination between employer and employee, thus if the illicit or negligent act was practiced by the employee in the exercise of typical activity given by the employer, it will be characterized the secondary strict liability of the employer by the harm caused to third parties. It is also relevant, thus the notion of work normality, which implies that the harmful act performed by the employee has temporal and local connection to the acts performed due to the employer's orders.[132]

114. The characterization of the employer's strict liability for the acts of his/hers employers is given by the demonstration of: (a) the practice of an illicit act by the employee founded in intent or fault; (b) the existence of a harm caused to a third party, that derives from an illicit practiced by the employee; (c) the existence of an dependence or subordination relationship between the employee and the employer; (d) that the employee has committed an illicit act in the exercise of his/her

130. See DIAS, Da Responsabilidade Civil, 2006, Rio de Janeiro, at 761–762, and CAVALIERI FILHO, Programa de Responsabilidade Civil, 2012, São Paulo, at 200–203.
131. Decree-Law nº 5.452, of May 1st, 1943.
132. See STOCO, Tratado de Responsabilidade Civil, 2014, São Paulo, at 1285–1286 and 1289–1290, and GONÇALVES, Responsabilidade Civil, 2006, São Paulo, at 145–146.

functions.[133] It is admitted the employer's obligation to pay damages extinction by proving that the harmful act was practiced beyond the employee's attributions. Furthermore, are applicable in these cases the illicit link breaks such as legitimate defense, the strict performance of right and the destruction or ruin of other's thing, removal of imminent harm (Article 188 of the Civil Code); the causation link breaks: act of god, fortuity, other's fact and victim's exclusive negligence (concepts constructed by doctrine and jurisprudence); as the reduction of damaged by contributory negligence (Article 945 of the Civil Code).[134]

115. It is vast the Brazilian jurisprudence in employer's liability by harms caused by their employees or servers, from the most common cases such as: traffic accidents caused by the employee driving a company's car;[135] physical injuries/death caused by an employee by securing the firm,[136] and; moral harms caused by an employee linked to illicit conducts performed in the working place, such as mobbing/bullying, sexual harassment and gender, race and religious prejudice.[137]

§2. Independent Contractors

116. In the Article 932, III, combined with Article 933, both from the Civil Code, it is predicted the secondary strict liability from the principal from the harms caused by its agent. It is qualified as principal "a person who charges another to buy, sell or practice any other act under his/her orders by his/her account, through some remuneration, named as commission," and as agent "any person hired to practice material acts by account of the principal."[138] It is essential to the characterization of the agency relation the establishment of a functional relationship, either permanent or transitory, among the principal and agent, being the acts practiced by the agent bonded to the direction and profit of the principal.[139]

117. Many contractual relationships can be framed as agency relationships for the appliance of secondary strict liability according to the terms of the Article 932, III, of the Civil Code, such as: mandate contract (Article 653 of the Civil Code, "whenever one receives from other powers to by its name practice acts or manage interests"); the commission contract (Article 693 of the Civil Code, "the contract of commission has by its object the acquisition or selling of goods by the

133. See DINIZ, Curso de Direito Civil Brasileiro, Responsabilidade Civil, 2009, São Paulo, at 539–540.
134. See CAVALIERI FILHO, Programa de Responsabilidade Civil, 2012, São Paulo, at 203–204.
135. STJ, 4ª Turma, REsp nº 1135988-SP, Relator Ministro Luis Felipe Salomão, DJe Oct. 17, 2013. Brasília.
136. STJ, 3ª Turma, AgRg no AREsp nº 315871-MT, Relator Ministro Sidnei Beneti, DJe Jun. 21, 2013. Brasília.
137. TST, 6ª Turma, AIRR nº 1203-74.2012.5.02.0008, Relator Ministro Augusto César Leite de Carvalho, DEJT 14.11.2014; TST, 3ª Turma, AIRR nº 1211-34.2013.5.03.0058, Relator Ministro Maurício Godinho Delgado, DEJT 22.05.2015; TST, 5ª Turma, RR - 831-24.2012.5.09.0011, Relator Ministro Emmanoel Pereira, DEJT 15.05.2015. Brasília.
138. See SILVA, Vocabulário Jurídico, 2008, Rio de Janeiro, at 184.
139. See WALD, Obrigações e Contratos, 2009, São Paulo, at 380.

commissionaire in his own name for the commitment"); the agency/distribution contract (Article 710 of the Civil Code, "by agency contracts, a person takes, in an non-eventual character, in addition to none dependence bounds, the obligation to promote, to other, through retribution, the fulfillment of certain business, in determined zone, characterizing the distribution, when the agent has in his/her power the thing to be negotiated"), and; the business agency contract (Article 722 of the Civil Code, "through the business agency contract, one who is not bonded to other through mandate, services or other dependence relationship of any kind obliges himself/herself to another one or more business, according to the received instructions").

118. On the other hand, the theme of independent contractors has arisen many controversies among other relationships, such as services relations (Article 593 and followings of the Civil Code) and in contractual relationships of journey (Article 610 and followings of the Civil Code).[140] The lack of labor or agency relation, in theory, does not authorize the appliance of secondary strict liability of Article 932, III, of the Civil Code, among these contractual relationships. However, it must be noted a tendency of appliance of agency notions by the jurisprudence to them. The Superior Court of Justice (Superior Tribunal de Justiça) has manifested itself in the sense that "it is not needed to be an typical labor contract; it is enough the dependence relationship or that one performs services for the interests or orders of another,"[141] being used the secondary strict liability of the principal for the acts of his/her agents in hypothesis such as: failure in the services performance by a doctor part of a clinical body of an hospital;[142] traffic accident caused by a driver ordered by the vehicle's owner,[143] and; illicit acts practiced by a priest or other members parts of religious institutions.[144]

§3. Liability of Legal Entities for Acts of Their Organs

119. Unlike what happens in the other hypothesis of vicarious liability or liability for acts of others in strict sense, regulated by the Civil Code in the Book I – Obligation's Law, Articles 932 and 933, the firm liability by acts of their organs is regulated by the Book II – Firm Law, in Articles 1.175 and 1.178 of the Civil Code. In the terms of the Article 1.175, the firm responds by the acts practiced by its manager, for he/her is considered "the permanent agent in the exercise of the firm, in its headquarters, office, branch or agency" (Article 1.172), which its functions are organized by the direction of labor in one of these physical establishments, exercising

140. See, GONÇALVES, Responsabilidade Civil, 2006, São Paulo, at 147.
141. STJ, 4ª Turma, AgRg no REsp 1020237-MG, Relator Mininstro Luis Felipe Salomão, DJe 29.06.2012. Brasília.
142. STJ, 3ª Turma, AgRg no Ag nº 1402439-RS, Relator Ministro Paulo de Tarso Sanseverino, DJe 10.04.2012. Brasília.
143. STJ, 4ª Turma, AgRg no AREsp nº 287935-SP Relator Ministro Luis Felipe Salomão, DJe 27.05.2014. Brasília.
144. STJ, 3ª Turma, REsp 1393699-PR, Relatora Ministra Nancy Andrighi, DJe 24.02.2014. Brasília.

the boss role among the organizational firm structure. In addition, in the terms of Article 1.178 caput, the firm is liable, by the acts practiced by any agent "practiced in its establishments related to the firm activities, even that they are not formally authorized," though, in the terms of Article 1.178's paragraph, "when such acts are practiced outside the establishment, it will only bound the principal the acts performed in the limits of powers given by documentation." Therefore, the entrepreneur, legal or natural person, is liable by the acts of any his/her agents, being irrelevant the nature of the obligational bound between them, since the acts are made inside the firm establishment and is related to the firm's activities, even if its performance was not authorized expressly and formally. However, the entrepreneur will only be obliged by the business acts practiced by the agent outside the establishment in the limits of the powers by him given to the agent in written documents.[145]

145. See CAMPINHO, O Direito da Empresa à luz no Novo Código Civil, 2010, Rio de Janeiro, at 373.

Chapter 2. Liability of Parents, Teachers and Instructors (for Children, Minors, and Students)

120. In Article 932, I, combined with Article 933, both from the Civil Code, is the secondary liability to parents for the harms caused by the acts performed by their underage children under their authority and surveillance. The source of this liability lies in the legal duty of surveillance of parents regarding their children, which spins off the familiar power established in Article 1.630 and followings of the Civil Code, which imposes to the parents many obligations, along with the duty to assist materially and morally their children as to survey and ward them.[146]

121. In the application of Article 932, I of the Civil Code, along with the traditional elements of the civil liability for the fact of others, it is necessary to combine two specific elements to them, such as the children's underage, and a factual circumstance in which the children is under his/her parents ward. If, by a legal or legitimate reason, such as divorce or separation of the parents, adoption by other, or legal emancipation of the children by marriage, occurs the rupture of familiar power, the parents are free from liability by the harms occurred by the acts of their underage children.[147] On the other hand, the parents are not free from liability in case of voluntary emancipation of the children,[148] if the children are not living with the parents,[149] or if the children are out of the parents living environment without a legal or legitimate reason that cast the parents ward out.[150] The Brazilian jurisprudence has recognized the secondary strict liability of parents by the damages caused by the acts of underage children in many situations, being the most common body injuries or death caused by traffic[151] or caused by gun fired by an underage person.[152]

122. In Article 932, II, combined with the Article 933, both from the Civil Code, is predicted the secondary strict liability of the tutor and curator by the harms caused by the tutored and the curate under their authority and ward. The source of this liability lies in the legal duty of care of the tutor, which legally represents the underage children who their parents are deceased, have disappeared, or were cast out of their familiar power, predicted in the Article 1.728 and followings of the Civil Code; and in the surveillance duty of the curator, who legally represents the incapable underage due infirmity, mental illness, madness, deafness, toxic-addiction or

146. See CAVALIERI FILHO, Programa de Responsabilidade Civil, 2012, São Paulo, at 195.
147. See PEREIRA, Responsabilidade Civil, 2012, Rio de Janeiro, at 125–126.
148. STJ, 4ª Turma, AgRg no Ag 1239557-RJ, Relator Ministra Maria Isabel Gallotti, DJe 17.10.2012. Brasília.
149. STJ, 3ª Turma, AgRg no AREsp 220930-MG, Relator Mininstro Sidnei Beneti, DJe 29.10.2012. Brasília.
150. See PEREIRA, Responsabilidade Civil, 2012, Rio de Janeiro, at 127.
151. STJ, 4ª Turma, REsp 1074937-MA, Relator Mininstro Luis Felipe Salomão, DJe 19.10.2009. Brasília.
152. STJ, 3ª Turma, REsp 777327-RS, Relator Mininstro Massami Uyeda, DJe 01.12.2009. Brasília.

prodigality of the curate, predicted in the Article 1.767 and followings of the Civil Code.[153]

123. The tutor and curator's situation is very much akin to the parents, namely, they respond for the acts practiced by the tutored and curate in the same legal conditions in which parents do for their children. Therefore, in general, are applied to tutors and curators the same principles that parents are subjected. The only relevant distinction in this matter is the right of redress, which, in the terms of Article 934 of the Civil Code, is possible for tutors and curators and forbidden to parents. The torts rule for parents, tutors and curators is established in the caput and paragraph of Article 928 of the Civil Code, which predicts the subsidiary and contributory liability of a private person, capable for the civil acts in relation to one who is under his/her ward: "the incapable responds to the harms it may cause, if the people for them responsible does not have the obligation to do it or does not have resources enough to," being the damage "not taking place if deprives of the necessary the incapable or the persons that depends on them."[154]

124. In Article 932, IV, combined with Article 933, both from the Civil Code, is predicted the secondary strict liability of hotel, bed and breakfast, houses or establishments where one finds housing for money, even for educational purposes, for the damages caused by their guests, inhabitants or students. This liability lies in the contractual duty of surveillance of educational institutions, hotels and establishments of this kind, such as mental institutions, kindergartens, nursing homes, etc. regarding their students, guests and inhabitants. It is fundamental to the secondary strict liability of this kind that the establishment receives payment in money for the services provided, otherwise, free housing is liable through negligence, according to Article 927, caput of the Civil Code.[155] As the educational and housing institutions are also services providers, they are subjected to the secondary strict liability rules of the Civil Code, as well as the strict liability predicted in the Article 14 of the Consumer's Protection Code,[156] according to the unanimous rational of the Superior Court of Justice (Superior Tribunal de Justiça).[157]

125. Regarding the educational institutions, it is due that they respond by the harms caused by the acts of their students, while practiced as students, which means, they respond for the acts of them while in the dependences of the educational institution of outside it while under the surveillance of their teachers and professors and other educators connected to the educational institution. The most frequent situations of this kind are harms caused by the students to the physical and moral

153. See GONÇALVES, Responsabilidade Civil, 2006, São Paulo, at 142–143, and CAVALIERI FILHO, 2010, São Paulo, at 198–199.
154. See FARIAS, BRAGA NETTO and ROSENVALD, Novo Tratado de Responsabilidade Civil, 2015, São Paulo, at 611–615.
155. See NADER, Curso de Direito Civil – Responsabilidade Civil, Saraiva, 2014, São Paulo, at 178–179.
156. See Part III, Ch. 3. Liability for Service.
157. STJ, 4ª Turma, REsp 762075-DF, Relator Minintro Luis Felipe Salomão, DJe 26.09.2009, and; STJ, 3ª Turma, REsp 1376460-RS, Relator Marco Aurélio Bellizze, DJe 30.09.2014. Brasilia.

integrity of other students. Less frequent, but due are harms caused from students to educators and other employees of educational institutions or to others.[158]

126. As for hotels and other shelter institutions, it can be verified that these responds for harms caused by their guests, but only while in the condition of guests, namely, in the dependences of the establishment or extended areas such as parking and pool dependences. In this category are framed harms caused to other guests, employees, and others.[159]

158. See GONÇALVES, Responsabilidade Civil, 2006, São Paulo, at 158–161.
159. See FARIAS, BRAGA NETTO and ROSENVALD, Novo Tratado de Responsabilidade Civil, 2015, São Paulo, at 629–631.

Chapter 3. Liability for Things and Animals

127. The Brazilian System of Torts regulates the liability for things and the liability for animals in specific normative articles. The Civil Code discipline the liability for things in Article 937, as harms caused by constructions or buildings in ruin, and in Article 938, the harms caused by throwing things fallen from buildings. The liability for animals is predicted in Article 936 of the Civil Code. In addition, by doctrinaire and jurisprudential construction, it is applied the thing's ward theory which widens the applicable spectrum of the duty of care to things or animals potentially harmful.

128. In the terms of Article 937 of the Civil Code, "the owner of a building or construction responds for the harm that results from its ruin, if they result from a lack of repair and necessity is due." As a natural consequence from the power exercise over a thing (Article 1.228 of the Civil Code), the owner of a building or construction should make the due repairs in buildings, aiming to not let it ruin and consequently cause harms to third parties. The expression ruin is admitted in a broad sense, absorbing the concept of complete or partial building destruction, as its parts such as tiles, glasses, marquees, insulating material, and others. The expression building also is admitted in a broader sense, encompassing the construction of walls, bridges, bypasses, lamppost, channels, elevators, escalators, and others.[160]

129. In the terms of Article 938 of the Civil Code, "one, who inhabits a building, or part of it, responds for the harm caused by things fallen or thrown from it to in an inappropriate place." One who is under the ward or occupation of a building or part of it, either as its owner, renter, enjoyer, or bailee, is liable by the harms caused to other for things fallen or thrown from his/her building. The legal text can be extensively interpreted, encompassing, not only housing buildings, but also commercial buildings such as offices, stores, event centers, among others.[161] In regard to the horizontal or vertical condominium, it will be considered liable in the hypothesis of not being verified in the unity where the object came from, according to the Superior Court of Justice (Superior Tribunal de Justiça),[162] it is an application of the alternative causation, being the obligation to pay damages allocated to the condominium.

130. As consolidated by the doctrinaire and jurisprudential rationale, regarding the Article 937 of Civil Code, the total or partial building ruin's liability (if the building itself falls, totally or partially, or things that are part of the building are

160. See NADER, Curso de Direito Civil, Responsabilidade Civil, 2014, Rio de Janeiro, at 199–201, and; DINIZ, Curso de Direito Civil Brasileiro, Responsabilidade Civil, 2009, São Paulo, at 558–559.

161. See NADER, Curso de Direito Civil, Responsabilidade Civil, 2014, Rio de Janeiro, at 206–207, and; STOCO, Tratado de Responsabilidade Civil, 2014, São Paulo, at 1304–1305.

162. STJ, 4ª Turma, REsp 64.682-RJ, Relator Ministro Bueno de Souza, DJ 29.03.1999, p. 180. Brasília.

detached), and Article 938 of the Civil Code, about the thrown or fallen things from buildings (objects that does not integrate the building, but have fallen or thrown from it) constitute modalities of strict liability for things, as a consequence of the risk theory. Therefore, it is needed only the harm and causation characterization to originate the obligation to pay damages, being unnecessary any analysis about the diligence or due care of the ruin or source of fallen or thrown things building's owner. The defenses of force majeure, act of God, third fact and the exclusive fault of the victim are admitted.[163]

131. In the terms of Article 936 of the Civil Code, "the owner or detainer of an animal will pay damages for the harms caused by it, if not being proved the victims own fault or act of god." Usually, as a natural consequence of the dominium power over a thing (Article 1.228 of the Civil Code), a liability for animals is due to the owner, detainer of the command and direction power over the animal. However, the owner can transfer the command and direction power over the animal to a third party, situation, where the liability for animals will reach the animal's current detainer. It is what happens, for instance, when the owner transfers the Ward over a domestic animal to a clinic, hotel, or veterinary hospital, or when the owner transfers the ward over a horse to a stud farm or horse society. Therefore, it is fundamental to the appliance of the legal hypothesis, the verification of who had the ward over the animal in the moment in which the facts had occurred.[164] The legal text is applicable to domestic/tamed and savage animals in captivity as, for example, in a circus or a zoo, and not being applicable to wild animals that have no legal bound of possession or ownership.[165] Among the diverse hypothesis of application of the legal rule, are: injuries caused by enraged dogs or savage animals kept in captivity; crops destruction or property harms caused by domestic animals, and; traffic accidents caused by animals' invasion on roads.[166]

132. According to the doctrinaire and jurisprudential mainstream rationale, the Article 936 of Civil Code of 2002, establishes the strict liability for animals, derived from the risk theory, therefore, it is enough to characterize the harm and causality between the animal behavior and the harm for the obligation to pay damages emerges for the owner or detainer of the animal. It is unnecessary, thus, any question about the due diligence or care by the owner or detainer during their wars on the animal.[167] It is admitted, by express legal disposition, the causation excludes of

163. See CAVALIERI FILHO, 2010, São Paulo, at 220, 234 and 236, and; STOCO, Tratado de Responsabilidade Civil, 2014, São Paulo, at 1301, 1307 and 1314.
164. See FARIAS, in: Rodrigues Junior, Mamede e Rocha, Responsabilidade Civil Contemporânea, 2011, São Paulo, at 207–208.
165. See CAVALIERI FILHO, Programa de Responsabilidade Civil, 2010, São Paulo, at 229.
166. See GONÇALVES, Responsabilidade Civil, 2006, São Paulo, at 278–282.
167. See CAVALIERI FILHO, Programa de Responsabilidade Civil, São Paulo, 2010, at 228–229; STOCO, Tratado de Responsabilidade Civil, São Paulo, 2015, at 1316–1317, and; SCHEREIBER, Novos Paradigmas da Responsabilidade Civil, São Paulo, 2009, at 32. On the other hand, assuming that the rule laid down in Art. 936 of the 2002 Civil Code is the negligence with presumption of guilt, see NADER, Curso de Direito Civil, Responsabilidade Civil, Rio de Janeiro, 2014, at 189, and; DINIZ, Curso de Direito Civil Brasileiro, Responsabilidade Civil, São Paulo, 2009, at 551.

act of god and victims exclusive own fault. Therefore, the owner or detainer of the animal can be free or liability if proves that the harm occurred by an unpredictable external fact or by the victims own fault, as, for instance, if the victim provokes the animal or have an imprudent behavior towards it.[168]

168. See FARIAS, in: Rodrigues Junior, Mamede e Rocha, Responsabilidade Civil Contemporânea, 2011, São Paulo, at 209.

Part III. Forms of Strict Liability

133. It is a contemporary phenomenon, the existence of a dualistic system of tort law, performing the coexistence of the basic rule of negligence, raised to the position of general principle of liability, with the rule of strict liability, applicable in cases specially provided for in all legal systems.[169] Under the rule of negligence, the agent responds for illicit acts, that constitute the obligation to pay damages due the guilty/negligence of one for the harm caused, being necessary to the emergence of this obligation, the convergence of three elements: the negligent act, the harm and causation. Under the rule of strict liability, the obligation emerges despite the negligence of the agent, who is bounded by a legal fact described in the normative system as source of liability, along with the presence of harm and causality relation.[170]

134. Considering the traditional legal doctrine, the application of strict liability is usually based on reasons such as: the imperative of social politics, specially public peace and social welfare; the standard term of equity; the abuse of rights, characterized by the exercise of rights by its owner with lack of respect for economic and social goals which are the reason for that right to be instituted or to use these rights harming the moral and good costumes, or even to exceed the limits of good faith; the guarantee theory, built on the duty of care imposed to special people such as parents for their children, employers for their employees; and, above them all, the risk theory.[171] Considering the law and economics theory (models of unilateral and bilateral causation, analyzing factors such as level of care, level of activity, level of information, risk distribution, and administrative costs), in general lines, strict liability is appointed as an efficient mechanism of control of the level of risk activity developed by the injurer, since it induces the internalization of social costs and reduces the level of activity to the socially optimal level.[172]

169. See DAM, European Tort Law, 2006, Oxford, at 256; WERRO, PALMER e HAHN, Strict Liability in European Tort Law: an Introduction, in WERRO and PALMER, The Boundaries of Strict Liability in European Tort Law, 2004, Durham, at 473.
170. See PEREIRA, Responsabilidade Civil, 1998, Rio de Janeiro, at 35.
171. See, PAULA, As excludentes de Responsabilidade Civil Objetiva, São Paulo, 2007, at 16–30.
172. See SCHAEFFER, Hand-Bernd and MÜLLER-LANGER, Strict Liability versus Negligence, in: BOUCKAERT and DE GEEST, Encyclopedia of Law and Economics, 2009, Cheltenham, at 3–45; and, BATTESINI, Direito e Economia, Novos Horizontes no Estudo da Responsabilidade Civil no Brasil, 2011, São Paulo, at 125–182.

135. In a comparative perspective, it can be verified that the contemporary Torts systems have all strict liability rules, focusing on the harms caused instead of the agent's negligence, as occurs in Environment Liability and the causation of damages as in animal's facts liability, transport liability, dangerous products liability and industry liability.[173] In addition, according to the degree of participation of the Judiciary in the application of strict liability, the legal systems can be classified as: open systems, in which it is competence of the Judiciary the task of defining the list of activities to apply strict liability, whose typical example is the United States; closed systems, in which the definition of the list of activities is an attribution of the Legislative, and to the Judiciary is not allowed to qualify activities to apply strict liability, whose typical example is Germany; and mixed systems, in which, besides applying strict liability to the list of activities prepared by the Legislative, the Judiciary has express legislative authorization to expand the list of activities, as is the case of Brazil.[174]

136. In many ways, the Brazilian Tort Law's system follows the French civil law tradition. Brazil has a dualist system of liability, which combines the negligence as the basic rule of negligence (Article 186 combined with Article 927, caput, of the Civil Code), with strict liability, focusing on the cause of the harm and the presence of the harm itself, being regulated by specific statutes, by the Federal Constitution of 1988, and by the Civil Code of 2002. Following this rational, are emblematic the manifestations of two major Brazilian jurists, namely Caio Mário da Silva Pereira,[175] author of the Draft Code of Obligations, in reforming the Brazilian Civil Code of 1916, and Miguel Reale,[176] the General Coordinator of the Commission responsible for preparing the Brazilian Civil Code of 2002. Pereira highlights that the two regimes coexist, negligence represents the basic notion and the general principle of liability based in negligence and strict liability is applied in cases specified by law, or when the injury comes from the situation created by an operator profession or activity which exposed the victim to the risk of harm. Miguel Reale states that "both forms of liability are intertwined and makes themselves thereby dynamics," thus should be recognized "negligence as the main rule, therefore the individual should be liable predominantly by its action or omission due its negligence or illicit will," which "does not exclude that the structure of business could lead to the strict liability … , this is a fundamental point."

173. See KOCH & KOZIOL, Comparative Conclusions, in KOCH and KOZIOL, Unification of Tort Law: Strict Liability, 2002, The Hague, at 395–406.
174. See BATTESINI, Comparative Tort Law and Economics: Strict Liability in Brazilian Legal Practice, 2013, New York, SSRN, at 21, http://ssrn.com/abstract=2263506.
175. See PEREIRA, Instituições de Direito Civil, 2008, Rio de Janeiro, at 562–563.
176. See REALE, Diretrizes Gerais sobre o Projeto de Código Civil, in REALE, Estudos de Filosofia e Ciência do Direito, 1978, São Paulo, at 176–177.

Chapter 1. Road and Traffic Accidents

137. As occurs in the US and UK,[177] the Traffic Law Torts System in Brazil is based in negligence, predicted in the Article 186, combined with Article 927, caput, of the Civil Code, it is up to the victim to prove the negligence of the defendant, the harm caused and the causation that binds the harm and the defendant.[178] It is broadly spread the theory of negligence versus the legality rule, which predicts that the express legal or normative duty is contradicted there is a presumption of negligence.[179] About that, are of fundamental importance the conduct and circulation norms predicted by the Brazilian Traffic Code (Lei n. 9.503/97), which acts as standards of comparison to factual negligent behavior. In case of traffic accidents are applicable: the illicit link breaks, legitimate self-defense, the regular exercise of right, the destruction or deterioration of other's thing or nuisance to avoid imminent harm (Article 188 of the Civil Code); the causation link break of fortuity, act of god and third party fact as victim's exclusive negligence; as the reduction of the damages by contributory negligence.

138. It is wide the Brazilian jurisprudence of traffic accidents,[180] concerning roads and street level accidents, accidents between vehicles, vehicle damages to pedestrian and bicycle riders, accidents triggered by bad road conditions, by bad signing, presence of animals and objects in the pavement, mechanic failures and mainly by negligent/ imprudent misconduct by riders breaching the traffic rules. Researches had estimated that 98% of accidents are caused due negligence/ imprudence of conductors, being the most common causes the excessive speed, use of cellphones during the ride, drunk drivers and a general disrespect of rules of defensive driving. Brazil has one of the largest death rates by traffic accidents in the world, 23.6 deaths per 100,000 inhabitants (2012), being registered 45,689 deaths and 177,487 accident related injuries by accidents in 2012.[181] This data is alarming and has triggered discussions about the efficacy of public policies in accident preventions and, in the field of Torts, it has justified doctrinaire positions that sustain the necessity of the use of strict liability in some situations,[182] either due direct application by the judiciary through the general clause of strict liability for risk activities stated in Article 927, paragraph of the current Civil Code or, as occurs in other countries of Civil Law as France and Germany, through specific legislation bonded with mandatory insurance.[183]

177. See KOCH & KOZIOL, Comparative Conclusions, in KOCH and KOZIOL, Unification of Tort Law: Strict Liability, 2002, The Hague, at 399.
178. See COELHO, Curso de Direito Civil – Responsabilidade Civil, 2005, São Paulo, at 329.
179. See CAVALIERI FILHO, Programa de Responsabilidade Civil, 2012, São Paulo, at 43.
180. See STOCO, Tratado de Responsabilidade Civil, 2014, São Paulo, at 1887–2117.
181. See OBSERVATÓRIO NACIONAL DE SEGURANÇA VIÁRIA – ONSV, Retrato da Segurança Viária no Brasil, 2014. Brasília, disponível em http://onsv.org.br.
182. See BATTESINI, Direito e Economia, Novos Horizontes no Estudo da Responsabilidade Civil no Brasil, 2011, São Paulo, at 246–247.
183. See KOCH & KOZIOL, Comparative Conclusions, in KOCH and KOZIOL, Unification of Tort Law: Strict Liability, 2002, The Hague, at 400.

139. In fact, the presence of a mandatory insurance for automobile vehicle owners (DPVAT), established by Law 6.194/74, is another characteristic trace of the Brazilian Torts system in traffic accidents. In addition to the conventional voluntary insurance of civil liability, the vehicle owner, in the moment of the vehicle's license expedition or renewal, is obliged to acquire an insurance favoring third parties as potential accident victims. In fact, the risks related to vehicles circulation are so expressive that the Brazilian legislator has established the mandatory insurance DPVAT a mean to guarantee a minimum compensation to accident victims (hospital, death, or permanent invalidity condition expenses) despite the conductor's negligence.

Chapter 2. Product Liability

140. The Product Liability in Brazil is regulated in the Consumer's Defense Code, Law 8.078/90, among the general rules of the Civil Code of 2002. In giving content to the Article 5, XXXII, of the Federal Constitution, the Brazilian legislator, with notable influences of the Resolution 39/248, de 09.04.1985, of the General Assembly of the United Nations and the European Union Directives 84/450 and 85/374, of 25.07.1985,[184] has promulgate the Consumer's Defense Code, in vigor since September 11th, 1990. In the elucidative expression of Sérgio Cavalieri Filho,[185] the Consumer's Defense Code has created a "super multidisciplinary legal structure, legal norms applicable to all Law's branches where there are consumption relations." In addition to the wide application field, the Consumer's Defense Code is known for being a law edified through principles and general clauses, which evokes the principles of strict good faith (Article 4, III), prevention (Article 6, VI), full compensation (Article 6, VI), information (Article 6, III), and rule of law (Article 12, paragraph 1). Another strong mark of the Consumer's Defense Code is the fact that it concentrates the notion of consumption relations and product circulation (Article 3, paragraph 1) as services circulation (Article 3, paragraph 2), establishing regulatory norms of general application, specific to product circulation and to services circulation.[186]

141. In essence, the civil liability in consumption relations occurs when either a product is defected and taken to the Market and therefore to the final consumer or when a product causes harm to the consumer. It is a contractual or extra-contractual legal relation that has in one pole the supplier and in the other the consumer in which the object is the circulation of products or services. The Consumer's Defense Code states the basic concepts of supplier, consumer, product and service. The legal definition of supplier is very wide, reaching all the participants in the productive-distributive cycle. It can be considered supplier "a physical or legal person, public or private, national or foreigner, as well of the depersonalized entities that are involved in production, assembling, importation, exportation, distribution or commercialization of products or services performance" (Article 3). The legal definition of consumer has as a structuring element the notion of final destination of the product, being considered as "consumer," "every physical or legal person who/which acquires a product or service as final destination" (Article 2). The Superior Court of Justice (Superior Tribunal de Justiça)[187] has consolidated the rational in the sense that there is not a consumption relation the acquisition of goods or services by a natural or legal person, whose goal is to implement or expand its core business, rejecting, therefore, the idea that its sufficient the existence of simple consumption act, independently of its finality. In addition to the direct consumer, the Consumer's

184. See BENJAMIN, Código de Defesa do Consumidor, 2011, São Paulo, at 1–8.
185. See CAVALIERI FILHO, Programa de Responsabilidade Civil, 2012, São Paulo, at 485–486.
186. The common regulatory rules and the specific rules of the circulation of products will be considered in this chapter and the specific regulatory rules of the service circulation will be considered in the next chapter.
187. STJ, 2ª Seção, REsp 541867-BA, Relator Ministro Antônio de Pádua Ribeiro, DJ 16.05.2005 p. 227. Brasília.

Defense Code also applies to the indirect consumer or consumer by extension, which is defined as "the collectivity of people, even that cannot be determined, that have interacted in consumption relations" (Article 2, single paragraph). The definition of product or services are object of express legal prediction. According to the Consumer's Defense Code, it can be considered product "any good, mobile or immobile, material or immaterial" (Article 3, paragraph 1) and consider services as "any activity given in the consumption Market, through remuneration" (Article 3, paragraph 2).

142. The Consumer's Defense Code adopts the system, which, *lato sensu*, works with two categories of defected product or services, distinguishing the product defect and fact. Product defects are less harmful misassembling that affects quality or quantity of products or services that makes them inadequate or inappropriate to consumption or could diminish its value, as disparities between the vessel, label, pack, or publicity indications and its content/ performance (Article 18, caput and Article 20, caput). Product or service facts are defects of major gravity that compromises the product safety that may cause harm to the consumer (Article 12, caput, and Article 14, caput). Both emerges from a defect of product or service, though while in defect stated by the CDC the harm is restricted to the product or service itself, that leads to malfunction, misuse or fruition and dysfunction, whereas in the product or services fact, the defect is so impacting that may cause external harm, as a consumption accident, that may inflict the consumer or third parties and cause to himself and/or others material or extra-material harm.[188] The solution given by the legislator to the products or services defect implies in the obligation of the supplier to end the defect or substitute the product/ re-execute the service or finally to restitute the product costs to the consumer, or proportionally discount the price of the product according to the consumers will (Article 18, paragraph 1, I, II, and III, and Article 20, caput, I, II, and III). To the product or services fact *stricto sensu*, the legislator has given a more severe regime, combining Tort Law rules to repair the harm caused to the consume and/or others due the consumption accident.

143. The supplier liability for products defect or fact *stricto sensu* is given by strict liability, which means that the supplier responds despite its negligent/ diligent behavior for the harm caused to consumers or others by the defective products release into the market. According to the Consumer's Defense Code, "the manufacturer, the producer, the constructor, national or Foreigner responds, independently of fault for the reparation of the harm caused to consumers, by defects from its Project, manufactory, construction, assembly, formulas, manipulation, presentation or storage of its products, as well as the information that may be insufficient or inadequate regarding its use or risks" (Article 12, caput). The strict liability of the production chain is joined. According to the Consumer's Defense Code, the manufacturer, the producer, the constructor and importer responds jointly for the release of the defected product in the market (Article 7°, paragraph, Article 18, caput, and Article 25, paragraphs 1 and 2). The strict liability of the merchant for

188. See CAVALIERI FILHO, Programa de Responsabilidade Civil, 2012, São Paulo, at 488.

the release of defected product, by its turn, is subsidiary, which means that the merchant responds to the consumer when the manufacturer, constructor, producer or importer cannot be identified or when the perishable products are not well conserved by the merchant himself (Article 13). It is secured the right of redress to one that was considered liable for by the consumer against the other participants of the industrial or service generation chain (Article 13, paragraph). The jurisprudence of the Superior Justice Court (Superior Tribunal de Justiça) has consolidated in the sense that the consumer can, by its choice exercise his pretention against the supplier of product or service that it's more convenient to him/her.[189]

144. For the application of strict liability of suppliers by fact or defect of product or services *stricto sensu* means, the Consumer's Defense Code consider defective the product that "does not offer the safety that its legitimately expected of it," regarding the relevant circumstances, namely: the product presentation (e.g., lack of user's manual, medicine leaflet, inadequate vessel, etc.); the use and risks that are reasonable expected (non-compliance to an reasonable expectation of the consumer); and, in an the time (available technology) in which the product was released (Article 12, paragraph 1, I, II, and III). According to the CDC (Article 12, caput), the product defects may be of conception (Project, creation, formula), production (construction, assembling, manipulation, manufacturing) or of market releasing (publicity, information, presentation, or storage). The product is not considered defective by the fact of other product of better quality to be placed in the market (Article 12, paragraph 2). In addition to the defect of product or service released in the market, the strict liability of the supplier in consumption accidents presupposes the causation nexus, the existence of material or immaterial harm caused to the consumer. The theme of the quantification of the moral harm in consumption accidents has triggered doctrinaire and jurisprudential controversies, meaning from the legislator's choice of not to establish a maximum or minimum limitations or the fixation of standard values for this kind of harm.[190]

145. The Consumer's Defense Code also predicts the liability exclusion causes for the supplier for defect of product or service, being these the causation excluding, for instance, of proving that he did not release the product in the market, that the defect does not exist, or that the fault is exclusive from the consumer or a third party (Article 12, paragraph 3, I, II, and III). The CDC predicts as well the causation excluding factors for product fact liability the proof of inexistence of defect, the victim's exclusive fault or a third party's exclusive fault (Article 14, paragraph 3, I and II). The application of the fortuity, act of god and development risk to consumption accidents, as they are not predicted in the CDC has brought doctrinaire and jurisprudential controversies,[191] being the Superior Court of Justice (Superior Tribunal de Justiça) positioned in favor to the appliance of these causality excluding

189. STJ, 3ª Turma, REsp nº 554.876-RJ, Relator Ministro Carlos Alberto Menezes Direito. Brasília.
190. See STOCO, Tratado de Responsabilidade Civil, 2014, São Paulo, at 634–635.
191. See STOCO, Tratado de Responsabilidade Civil, 2014, São Paulo, at 616–617 and 624.

factors.[192] Regarding the products or services that are embedded with risk due their own nature, quality or function (weapons, medicines with high risk rate, medicines with contraindications, agrotoxics, etc.), it is void the illicit conduct of the supplier in case of embedded risk, to one that releases them in the market, regarding the duty of information established in Article 9 of the CDC: "the supplier of products or services potentially harmful or dangerous to health or safety should inform in an ostensive and adequate manner about its harmfulness or danger." The reduction of the damages by contributory liability in consumption accidents is another theme of controversies between the doctrine and jurisprudence,[193] bring the Superior Court of Justice (Superior Tribunal de Justiça) in favor to the appliance of this institute, as states in Article 945 of the Civil Code.[194]

146. Agreeing and complementing the strict liability of the supplier for the fact or defect. Of products of the CDC, the Civil Code of 2002, has embodied in analogue fashion the strict liability of individual entrepreneurs and firms for harms caused by their products in circulation, stating that "aside other cases predicted in special laws, the individual entrepreneurs and firms respond despite fault by the harms caused by their products in circulation" (Article 931, of the Civil Code) It is an general clause of strict liability even more wide than the one predicted in the CDC (Article 12), thus the statement predicted in the Civil Code is applicable even when there is not an consumption relation, encompassing, therefore, a wider spectrum of accidents caused by defaced products released.[195]

147. In addition to the rules of civil liability of the supplier, the Consumer's Defense Code predicts instruments that are complementary to act in situation of risk in accidents of consumption and the defense of the consumer. In the code are also predicted administrative sanctions (Article 56, I to XII) and criminal sanctions (Articles 63–74), it also predicts the disregard of legal entity on firms that acts against the consumer, abuse of its rights, violates the law, statutes of the social contract, go bankrupt, be insolvent or shut its activities due bad administration (Article 28). The defense of interests of consumers and victims can be exercised individually or collectively (Article 81). The collective defense will be exercised when is case of interests or diffuse rights (trans-individuals, indivisible nature, of a group, category, or class of persons) and individual rights that are homogeneous (of common origin), being legitimate for the action proposition the Public Ministry, The Federal Union, the Estates, Municipalities, the Federal District, entities and branches of the Public Administration as defense of consumers associations (Article 81, paragraph, I to III, and Article 82, I to IV).

---

192. STJ, 3ª Turma, REsp nº 120.647/SP, Relator Ministro Eduardo Ribeiro, DJ 15.05.2000, p. 156. Brasília.
193. See CAVALIERI FILHO, Programa de Responsabilidade Civil, 2012, São Paulo, at 500.
194. STJ, 4ª Turma, REsp nº 287.849-SP, Relator Ministro Ruy Rosado do Aguiar, DJ 13.08.2001, p. 165. Brasília.
195. See FACCHINI NETO, A Responsabilidade Civil no Novo Código, Revista do Tribunal Superior do Trabalho, RS, v. 76, n. 1, p. 17–63, Jan./Mar. 2010, Porto Alegre, at 196.

Chapter 3. Liability for Service

148. It is wide the application field of the Consumer's Defense Code in matters of services circulation, comprehending, by express legal disposition, "any activity supplied in the consumption Market, trough remuneration, including the banking, financial, credit and insurance activities, aside those of labor nature" (Article 3, paragraph 2). The Superior Court of Justice (Superior Tribunal de Justiça) has consolidated the rational that the CDC is applicable to the financial institutions,[196] the private retirement entities[197] and health insurance contracts.[198] The public services, comprehending the water supply, electric supply, gas supply, telephonic services and public transportation, by express legal disposition also are submitted to the Consumer's Defense Code (Article 22, caput and paragraph).

149. The supplier liability for fact or defect of product or service *stricto sensu* is objective, which means that the supplier responds independently of fault by the harms caused to consumers by defective services released in the market. According to the Consumer's Defense Code, "the supplier of services responds, independently of the existence of fault, for the compensation of harms caused to consumers by defects related to the services performance, as well as for insufficient or inadequate information about its fruition and risks" (Article 14, caput). The strict liability of the participants of the generation of services chain, including the merchants, by the release of the defective service in the market is case of joint liability, bring secured the right of redress to one that was called by the consumer that can by his/her will evoke the supplier that is more convenient to him/her. In order to apply the strict liability of the supplier for fact of service or defect of service *stricto sensu*, the CDC consider defective the service that "does not supply the security that the consumer could expect taking in consideration the relevant circumstances," among: the method of supply; the result and risks that may be reasonable expected at the time of its release (Article 14, paragraph 1, I, II, and III). The service is not considered as defective by adoption of new techniques by the market (Article 14, paragraph 2).

150. Complementing the rule of strict liability of the supplier by facto of service of defect of service *stricto sensu* present in the CDC, the Civil Code states the strict liability of the transporter by the harms caused to persons and luggage,[199] establishing the "voidance of any clause that may exclude liability" (Article 734, caput, of the Civil Code).

151. In its strict liability system of supplier by the fact of the service or default service in the strict sense, the Consumer Code makes an exception for professionals, for which the liability is subjective. By express legal provision, "the responsibility of independent professionals shall be determined upon verification of guilt"

196. STJ, súmula 297. Brasilia.
197. STJ, súmula 321. Brasilia.
198. STJ, súmula 469. Brasilia.
199. STJ, 3ª Turma, AgRg no Ag nº 778.804/RJ, Relator Ministro Humberto Gomes de Barros, DJe 14.12.2007. Brasília.

(Article 14, paragraph 4). Therefore, considering the *nature intuitu personae* of the service provided by liberal professions, the Brazilian legislator opted for subjective responsibility of doctors, lawyers, engineers, dentists and other professionals,[200] making it necessary to check the fault, in line with Article 186 combined with Article 927, caput, of the Civil Code of 2002.[201]

200. See Part I, Ch. 2, §1. Liability of professionals.
201. In addition to the specific rules on the circulation of services covered in this chapter, look up common regulatory rules of the circulation of goods and services, dealt with in the previous chapter.

Chapter 4. Environmental Liability

152. The Environment Preservation is a fundamental value in Brazilian Society, it was even guarded as a Constitutional value (Article 170, VI of the Brazilian Federal Constitution). The Federal Constitution of 1988 establishes the ecologic and equilibrated environment "of common use of the people, essential to the healthy quality of life, obliging the Public Powers and the collectivity the duty of defending and preserve it to the present and future generations" (Article 225, caput). The constitutional text itself predicts a bundle of measures to the Public Powers destined to secure the preservation of the Environment (Article 225, paragraph 1, I–VII), stating tree spheres of sanctions for one who harms the environment, namely: the criminal, administrative and civil sanctions (Article 225, paragraph 3). In this particular, it is a fact that the Federal Constitution of 1988 has received the Law nº 6.938/81, the legal statement which established the National Defense of the Environment Policy, which contents rules of civil liability in environmental law, along with the constitution itself.

153. The National Policy of Environment Defense's Law (Lei de Política Nacional de Defesa do Meio Ambiente), has internalized the principle polluter pays of ECO92, as an instrument of control of the level of risk to the environment of an activity and the internalization of negative externalities of a firm or activity. It also internalizes the precautionary principle as an instrument to deter environmental damages, when there is no scientific proof that there is no meaningful harm to the environment in determinate activity and the precaution principle as a mean of strict liability connected to environmental damages in case of a probability of harm. As states the Article 14, paragraph 1, of the law 6.938/81, the polluter is "obliged, despite his negligence/diligence to pay damages to the environment and to third parties affected by his/her activity." The adoption of the strict liability takes aside the fault/negligence content of the discussion of the nature of the activity, though it doesn't cast aside the necessity of proof of the other two conditions of civil liability, namely, the causation nexus and the harm, though it may bring disputes in terms of doctrine and jurisprudence in the application of the principles of precaution and the precautionary principle.

154. The doctrine[202] and the jurisprudence[203] at large justify the strict liability in environmental damages through the integral risk theory, an extreme modality of the risk theory that admits the flexibility of the causation nexus burden of proof with the adoption of the theory of the antecedents equivalence instead of the adequate causation, as a mean to amplify the agents liable to give more efficacy to the compensation of environmental harms. In addition, the adoption of the integral risk theory, as comprehended by the Superior Court of Justice (Superior Tribunal de Justiça), can cast aside the causation nexus excluding factors as fortuity, act of god,

202. See PAULA, As excludentes de Responsabilidade Civil Objetiva, 2007, São Paulo, at 75.
203. STJ, 2ª Seção, REsp nº 1.354.536/SE, Relator Ministro Luis Felipe Salomão, DJe 05.05.2014. Brasília.

fact of third party and exclusive victims fault.[204] It is not less polemic the theme of the collective moral harm in doctrine[205] and jurisprudence[206] polarized between those who defend and those who reject its application in environmental law.

204. STJ, 3ª Turma, AgRg no REsp nº 1.412.664/SP, Relator Ministro Raul Araújo, DJe 11.03.2014. Brasília.
205. See STOCO, Tratado de Responsabilidade Civil, 2014, São Paulo, at 1182–1188.
206. See STJ, 2ª Turma, REsp 1.328.753/MG, Relator Herman Benjamin, DJe. 28.05.2013, and, STJ, 1ª Turma, REsp. 598.281/MG, Relator Ministro Teori Albino Zavaski, DJe 01.06.2006. Brasília.

Chapter 5. Others

155. In addition to the hypothesis analysed in the previous chapters, the strict liability in Brazil is established by specific statutes, along with the Constitution of 1988 and the Civil Code of 2002. The first law to predict the strict liability in Brazil is the Executive Act n. 2.681, December 7, 1912, which has regulated the rail road transportations, according to the activity risk theory, in its Article 26, makes liable "the rail roads for every harms that the exploration of their lines cause to marginal owners."[207] The liability excluding specific to rail roads is established in Article 26, paragraph: "it will cease, though, the liability if the harmful event is from direct cause of infraction by the owner, of legal statement or regulation related to buildings, plantations, excavations, material storage or animals ward in the boards of railroads."

156. In the Mining Code (Executive Law Act n. 227, February 28, 1967) lies another cause of strict liability in the Article 47, VIII, in which the owner of concession of a mining operation responds for "harms and losses to third parties, that result directly or indirectly of the exploration." The damages caused by the mining activity are, in essence environmental, situation in which, most part of situations cast aside causation excluding factors due the integral risk theory as seen in the prior chapter.

157. The strict liability is also predicted in the Brazilian Aeronautics Code (*Código Brasileiro de Aeronáutica*, Lei n. 7.565, December 19, 1986), in which, in its Article 268, turns liable the air transportation explorer for "the damages to third parties in surface, caused directly by flight or maneuver as person or thing fallen or projected by it." The liability excluding specific to air transportation are established in Article 268, paragraph 2º, I-IV, which are: the lack of direct cause and effect relation between the harm and the facts appointed; the fact of the harm result only of the passage of the flight through the airspace complying to the rules of air traffic; if the flight is operated by a third party or agent, or dependent that has exercised reasonable caution on the apparel and if there was configured exclusive victims fault.

158. The Federal Constitution of 1988 determines to be competence of the Federal Union the exploration of nuclear services and installations of any nature establishing in its Article 21, XXIII, "d," that the "civil liability for nuclear harms does not depend of existence of fault." The strict liability in nuclear activities is also regulated by the law nº 6.453, of October 17th, 1977, which in Article 4º, I–III, establishes that the nuclear installation responds independent of fault the reparation of nuclear harms, occurred in the installation or provoked by nuclear material origin or sent to the installation. The liability excluding factors specific to nuclear activities are established in Articles 6 and 8 of law 6.453, namely: that the damage

207. The vigency of the Executive Act n. 2.681, Dec. 7, 1912, in face to the promulgation of the Consumer's Defense Code and the Civil Code of 2002, is under discussion. See CAVALIERI FILHO, Programa de Responsabilidade Civil, 2012, São Paulo, at 147, and, DIAS, Da Responsabilidade Civil, 2006, Rio de Janeiro, at 597.

is resulted by victim exclusive's fault; and, that the damage may be caused directly by armed conflict, hostilities, civil war, insurrection, or exceptional fact of nature.[208]

159. Another hypothesis of strict liability with constitutional origin, is the strict liability of the State, established in the Article 37, paragraph 6: "the legal persons of public or private law that perform public services will respond by the harm caused by its agents, in this quality that may cause to third parties." In addition to the constitutional norm of Article 37, 6, the Civil Code of 2002 regulates the strict liability of the state in its Article 43, where "the legal persons of internal public law are liable civilly by their acts and their agents in this quality that may cause harm to third parties."[209]

160. The Civil Code of 2002 establishes the strict liability, along with other legal statutes that regulates specific cases. Regarding the services and products,[210] it states that: the strict liability of the transporter by harms caused to people and luggage transported is established in the Article 734; in addition, the strict liability of the entrepreneur by products in circulation is given by Article 931.

161. Regarding the indirect liability by the fact of others or vicarious liability,[211] the Civil Code of 2002 established that these are: the strict liability of parents for harm caused by the acts performed by their underage children, and the curator and tutor's liability for acts performed by their curate's and pupils in Article 932, I, combined with Article 933; the firm owner's liability or commitment by the acts of employees, servants and agents in Article 932, III, combined with Article 933; the strict liability of hotels, bed and breakfast, houses or establishments where one can find shelter from money owners for acts performed by their guests, tenants and students in Article 932, IV combined with Article 933; and the strict liability of persons who freely have participated in product of crimes until their quote of participation, by harms provided by the criminals in Article 932, V, combined with Article 933. The rule of the strict liability of parents, tutors and curators is given by the Article 928, caput and paragraph, which predicts the subsidiary and mitigated liability of one deprived of rational to the practice of acts of civil life (persons under the age of 16, persons who are ill, and persons with mental illnesses) in regard to the persons that took them under their guard: "the incapable responds for the harm he/she may cause, if the people who are responsible for him/her ate not obliged to make it or don't have the resources to pay the damages," and the damages "will not

208. The application of the excluding factors established by the Arts 6 and 8 of law 6.453 of 1977 after the Federal Constitution of 1988, with the receiving of the integral risk theory is a controversial matter. See PAULA, As excludentes de Responsabilidade Civil Objetiva, 2007, São Paulo, at 83–86, and, STJ, 2ª Turma, REsp. 1180888/GO, Relator Ministro Herman Benjamin, DJe 28.02.2012. Brasília.

209. See Part I, Ch. 1, §2. Liability of public authorities (governmental liability).

210. See Part III, Ch. 2. Product Liability and Ch. 3. Liability for Service.

211. See Part II, Ch. 1. Vicarious Liability and Ch. 2. Liability of Parents, Teachers and Instructors (for Children, Minors, and Students).

take place if they deprive the incapable or people that depend of him of existence resources."

162. As for the indirect liability for act or facto f thing or animal or liability for things and animals,[212] the Civil Code establishes that: the strict liability by fact of animal is predicted in Article 936; the strict liability by ruin and construction in Article 937; and the, strict liability by harm caused by fallen or tossed things from buildings in Article 938.

163. In addition to establish the strict liability in normative statutes that regulates the specific hypothesis mentioned, the Civil Code also establishes the strict liability through general clauses with open content. The abuse of rights,[213] qualified in Article 187 as the exercise of a right with manifest excess according to the "limits imposed by its economic or social goals as well as the good Faith and good costumes," which leads to the strict liability of the owner of rights by the harms caused by the abusive act or omission.

164. One of the main innovations made by the Civil Code of 2002 is the general clause of strict liability by the activity risk provided by Article 927, paragraph, "there will be obligation to repair the harm caused, independently of fault, in cases specified in law, or when the activity regularly exercised by the harm's author implies, by its nature, in risks to rights of others."[214] Along with the general clause of strict liability for dangerous activities of the paragraph of Article 927, has expanded the courts possibilities of actuation significantly. The courts were explicitly authorized to qualify some activities as dangerous, therefore, making them subject for strict liability application. Thus, it is possible to say that, Brazil changes from a closed civil law system, as is the case of Germany, for a mixed civil law system, similar to Italy and Portugal, making significant progress in promoting the harmonious action of the Legislative and the Judiciary in the process of defining what activities are subject to strict liability.[215] Enlightening is the manifestation of Schreiber:[216]

> the general clause of strict liability directs itself to hazardous activities, which is to say; to activities that presents a high level of risk, either because they center themselves under intrinsically harmful goods (as radioactive, explosive and

---

212. See Part II, Ch. 3. Liability for Things and Animals.
213. See Part I, Ch. 2, §3. Abuse of rights.
214. In this particular, the Brazilian system of Torts is in line with institutes as the Principles of European Tort Law (Art. 5:101. abnormally dangerous activities), elaborated by the European Group on Tort Law, and the Restatement of the Law Third, Torts: Liability for Physical and Emotional Harm (§20. Abnormally Dangerous Activities), made by The American Law Institute. See BATTESINI, Comparison of Tort Law Systems from the perspective of economic efficiency: Brazilian Civil Code, Principles of European Law and Restatements of the Law, New York, SSRN, 2015, at 7-8, http://ssrn.com/abstract=2595790.
215. See BATTESINI, Comparative Tort Law and Economics: Strict Liability in Brazilian Legal Practice, 2013, New York, SSRN, at 26, http://ssrn.com/abstract=2263506.
216. See SCHREIBER, Novos Paradigmas da Responsabilidade Civil, da Erosão dos Filtros da Reparação à Diluição dos Danos, 2009, São Paulo, at 25.

weaponry materials, etc.), or because they use methods of high harmful potential (as the control of hydrological resources, nuclear energy manipulation, etc. The definition, although elastic, of a list of activities covered in the application scope of the sole paragraph of the Article 927, is a task appointed to jurisprudential action and to doctrinaire investigations.

165. Being an open clause, the problem's core that presents itself to the judiciary is on the characterization of dangerous activities. In this context, the establishment of clear and objective directives acquire relevance, through the consideration of factors as the elevated probability of accidents rates, the magnitude of expected damages and the impossibility of avoidance of accidents, even though the adoption of adequate precautions implementation.[217] In applying the general clause of the Article 927, paragraph of the Civil Code, the jurisprudence has qualified as dangerous activities the generation and distribution of electric energy,[218] the construction of dams[219] and monetary values transportation.[220]

217. See BATTESINI, Direito e Economia, Novos Horizontes no Estudo da Responsabilidade Civil no Brasil, 2011, São Paulo, at 240–241.

218. STJ, 4ª Turma, REsp 896.568/CE, Relator Ministro Luis Felipe Salomão, DJ. 30.06.2009, p. 233. Brasília.

219. STJ, 4ª Turma, REsp 1374342/MG, Relator Ministro Luis Felipe Salomão, DJe. 25.09.2013. Brasília.

220. STJ, 3ª Turma, REsp 185659/SP, Relator Ministro Carlos Alberto Menezes Direito, DJ 18.09.2000 p. 126. Brasília.

Part IV. Defenses and Exception Clauses

Chapter 1. Limitation of Action (Suspension and Interruption)

166. Brazilian Law adopts, as a rule, the "whole reparation principle," which means that is "ideal to put the harm party in an equivalent situation as he/she was before the act."[221] This principle can be perceived "in its most broad dimension... when is considered the pecuniary damage,"[222] thus the losses must be estimated to compensate the harmed party as a whole. This principle is predicted in the caput of Article 944 of the Civil Code ("The damages are measured by the extension of the harm"), but it has its limitations.

167. The first of them can be extracted by the paragraph of the same Article 944, since it is established by it that "if there is an excessive disproportion between the fault degree and the damage, the judge can reduce by proportionally the damage." It is about to balance the whole reparation principle with the proportionality postulate, which derives, by its turn, from the notion of the broad sense of equity, and which, exceptionally, attributes importance and intensity to the responsible fault, which, also lets, "in a certain measure, a return to a prior stage of great, light and lightest fault."[223]

168. As states Sanseverino:[224]

> the main clause of damages reduction, predicted in the normative clause of the Article's 944 paragraph of the CC/2002, gives to the judge the power/duty to proceed an equitable solution, to the concrete scenario, in cases of the excessive disproportion between the agent fault's degree and the severity of the harms suffered by the victim for means to decide the amount of the damages, considering three distinctive elements, relevant in legal fact-related situations: (a) the fault's degree; (b) the extension of the harm; (c) the excessive disproportion between the fault and the damage.

221. See SANSEVERINO, Princípio da Reparação Integral, 2013, São Paulo, at 19.
222. *Ibid.*, at 49.
223. See DIREITO & CAVALIERI FILHO, Comentários ao Novo Código Civil, 2007, Rio de Janeiro, at 338.
224. See SANSEVERINO, Princípio da Reparação Integral, 2013, São Paulo, at 99.

As highlighted by the same author:

> the first element to be considered in terms of application of the general clause of damages reduction, is the harmful agent's fault. Differently of what happens with the Article 186 of the Civil Code, in which the intent and fault were considered the same for the configuration of the illicit purposes, the expression "fault" from the Article 944's paragraph must be taken in its strict sense *(culpa stricto sensu)*, not having the incidence of reduction regarding the intended acts.

As for the second aspect, "the harms suffered by the victim must be of a great amount, considering not only its objective extension, but also the economic value of the correspondent damages … " and "the nature of the harms suffered by the victim must also be considered, thus, if the harmed interests are only patrimonial, related to material harms provoked by the illicit (e.g., traffic accident provoked by light fault with extensive damages, though, only material), can be considered fully applicable the norm in question, as the its main *topei* the equity."[225] Finally, concerning the exigence of disproportion, states Sanseverino[226] that:

> the expression excessive disproportion, means that the disequilibria between the fault's degree and the extension of the harms must be logical, and what must be observed through the formulation of a reasonable judgement, which is the criteria to be used by the judge to proceed to reduction.

169. Another limitation may be found in the rule disposed in the paragraph of Article 928 of the Civil Code. In the caput, is predicted the civil liability of incapables, and furthermore, equity is evoked ("The damages predicted in this article must be equitable, and will not take place if deprives of the necessary means the incapable or persons that may depend on him/her"). It deserves a quote the fact that the "integral reparation principle" indicates, not only the called "compensatory function" (or "reparatory") of Tort Law, but also what Sanseverino[227] has called an "indemnitor function": "the extension of the harms constitutes the maximum limit to the damages." This aspect (limitation) of the Article 944 of the Civil Code's content takes a great portion of the Brazilian doctrine[228] to consider the punitive damages system incompatible with the Brazilian system. Though the matter is not considered pacified (there are positions in the contrary sense),[229] the reality is that

225. *Ibid.*, at 107.
226. *Ibid.*, at 107.
227. See SANSEVERINO, Princípio da Reparação Integral, 2013, São Paulo, at 59.
228. See MIRANDA, Tratado de direito privado, 2003, Campinas; SILVA, O dano moral e sua reparação, 1969, Rio de Janeiro; GONÇALVES, Direito civil brasileiro. Responsabilidade civil, 2010, São Paulo; THEODORO JUNIOR, Comentários ao novo código civil, 2003, Rio de Janeiro; MORAES, Danos à pessoa humana: uma leitura civil-constitucional dos danos extrapatrimoniais 2003, São Paulo; and, SANSEVERINO, Princípio da Reparação Integral, 2010, São Paulo.
229. See PEREIRA, Responsabilidade Civil, 2012, Rio de Janeiro; DINIZ, Curso de direito civil brasileiro. São Paulo, 2009; BITTAR, Responsabilidade civil: teoria e prática, 1990, Rio de Janeiro; CAVALIERI FILHO, Programa de responsabilidade civil, 2010, São Paulo; FIUZA, Direito

the "punitive damages" are admitted in practice by the Brazilian courts, by the establishment of non-pecuniary damages (or "moral damages"), without defined criteria (the appreciation is done in each case), under the argument of the "pedagogic function" of civil liability (in clear confusion with the deterrence function and the punitive function of the tort law).[230]

170. Other limitations to the full appliance of the generic norms of Civil Liability may be identified in cases of special immunities, spinning of the constitutional statements or special laws. It is the case of the parliamentary (caput of Article 53 of the Federal Constitution), which cannot be held defendants in civil (or criminal) law by their opinions, words and votes, defending the Supreme Court (Supremo Tribunal Federal)[231] that this limitation is restricted to the typical exercise of the activity of legislation. Other case of immunity is applied to attorneys, by their acts and manifestations in the exercise of their profession (Lei nº 8.906/94, Article 2º, §1º, and Article 7º, §2º), with the restrictions stated in the same legal document ("The Attorney's Statute/ *Estatuto da Advocacia*"). It is not rare, though, the immunities cases to be dismissed in situations of abuse of rights.[232] It is worth it to highlight that, in Brazilian Law, diplomatic immunities do not reach the Civil Liability realm.

---

civil. Curso completo, 2010, Belo Horizonte; ANDRADE, Dano moral e indenização punitiva: os punitive damages na experiência do common law e na perspectiva do direito brasileiro, 2009, Rio de Janeiro; and, VENTURI, Responsabilidade Civil Preventiva, 2014, São Paulo.

230. See SANTOLIM, Nexo de Causalidade e Prevenção na Responsabilidade Civil no Direito Brasileiro e Português. RIDB, Ano 3 (2014), nº 10, available at http://www.idb-fdul.com.
231. See STJ, HC nº 81.730, Relator o Ministro NELSON JOBIM, julgado em 01/08/2003. Brasília.
232. See Ch. 1, §4.

Chapter 2. Grounds of Justification

171. Must be taken into consideration, for the exclusion of civil liability, the hypothesis of legal business that expressively cast it out, situations of exemption clauses (necessity state, regular exercise of rights and self-defense) and cases of causation exemption (exclusive victim's fact, concurrent causation, third party's fact, fortuity, and act of god). It still deserves attention the statutory limitations, which is not specific to tort law, but also belongs to the efficacy realm.

§1. Consent

172. There is no specific provisions in the Brazilian Civil Code about the "non-solicitation clauses,"[233] which is "the stipulation from which one of the hiring parties declares, with the allowance of the other, that will not be liable by events of harm experienced by the first, resulting from the inexecution or inadequate execution of a contract, harm this, that, without the clause would be compensated to the party."[234] This situation is restricted to the contractual liability, which escapes from the object of this study. Even though, the illustration is worth to refer thus the great debate present in the Brazilian doctrine[235] and jurisprudence[236] about the validity of this clause. The cases in which there could be a "tacit consent" of the harmed party, takes place when, with a consideration of his/her behavior the harmed party contributes to the occurrence of the harmful fact; these cases will be studied in the light of the cases of "victim facts" furthermore.

§2. Exemption Clauses

173. According to the Article 188 of the Civil Code, "does not constitute illicit acts: I – the ones practiced in self-defense or in the regular exercise of a recognized right; II – the deterioration or destruction of other's thing, or harm to a person to remove imminent danger." In addition, the paragraph of the same article states that, "in the case of II, the act will be legal only while the circumstances are absolute necessary, not exceeding the limits indispensable for the of the danger's removal." The illicit exclusion, as a rule, excludes the civil liability, but, as seen before (Part

233. Which motivates the critiques of RODRIGUES, Direito Civil – vol. 4 – Responsabilidade Civil, 2002, São Paulo, at 182.
234. See RODRIGUES, *supra*, at 179.
235. See DIAS, Cláusula de não-indenizar, 1980, Rio de Janeiro.
236. There is no greater controversy about the theme of the consume relations, when the consumer is a natural person (the clause is considered invalid, due the disposition of the Art. 51, I, da Lei nº 8.078/90 – Consumer's Defense Code). As for the transportation contracts, the theme was subject of the Sumula 161 of the Supreme Federal Court ("In transportation contracts, is invalid the non-solicitation clause"). As for contracts in which there are none consumer relations, the jurisprudence has adopted contradictory positions (while against in Civil Appeal, Apelação Cível nº 2000000403415-1/000, of TJMG, it is favorable, as shown in the Civil Appeal, Apelação Cível nº 9145437-46.2005.8.26.0000, do TJSP).

I, §1), there may be civil liability even without illicit acts. Is what can be comprehended by the disposition of the Article 929 of the Civil Code, thus "if the harmed person, or the thing's owner, in the case of the II of Article 188, are not blamed by the danger, the damages for the harm suffered is due." Which means that: even if the act is licit (thus there was a preexclusion of the illicit nature), the civil liability will take place. The rule of Article 930 adds that "in the case of II of Article 188, if the danger occurs by fault of a third party, the author of the harm has the right of redress to compensate the damages paid to the harmed." Finally, in the paragraph of the same Article: "the same action will compete against one who in self-defense has caused the harm (Article 188, I)." In other words: the harmful act will be licit, but the agent must pay damages to the harmed (civil liability), with right of redress to the one who caused the danger or aggression, which has originated the self-defense.

I. Necessity State

174. The Necessity State is an exemption clause related to the 171, which limits the application ambit of civil liability in extreme cases where one, in order to prevent a great danger or harms to oneself of third parties inflicts harms to another. According to Theodoro Junior,[237]

> The necessity state occurs when a person involves oneself in a factual situation, in which, to get rid of a danger in motion, see oneself compelled to sacrifice another person or another person's thing. In the realm of interests, though licit the agent's conduct, it will be in some cases in conflict with also worthy interests of one who had to suffer the harm necessary to save the rights of the first. Even that the law states the licit act (lack of illicit), and it made it the Article 188, II, the agent will not be always free from the obligation to repair the harm to the one who suffered the consequences of the salvation act of person or thing under risk. Therefore, bring the victim the one, who gave cause to the danger, he/she will not be able to complain about the harm suffered to get rid of the risk created. But, if the person offended (owner of the harmed goods) did not contributed to the origin of the dangerous situation, the Code imposes to the agent the obligation to pay damages for the harmed, even though he/she acted to exercise right recognized by the legal order (Art. 929). It is not, though, through the illicit nature of the act that such liability will be imposed, but on the bases of the fact-act that the law values as good to solve an interests conflict. The duty to pay damages, in the Code's systematic does not emerges only from the illicit (Art. 927). Many other causes also generate the same liability, among them, the fact-acts and even simple licit facts.

175. The author also reminds that for "a legitimate reaction, authorized by the Article 188 take place, it is demanded from the agent to be put in an unavoidable alternative, to preserve one own thing through the sacrifice of another's."[238]

237. See THEODORO JUNIOR, Comentários ao Novo Código Civil, 2003, Rio de Janeiro, at 141.
238. See THEODORO JUNIOR, Comentários ao Novo Código Civil, 2003, Rio de Janeiro, at 143.

II. Due Use of Rights

176. As the "abuse of rights" defines an objective illicit hypothesis, as demonstrated (Part I, §4), the "due" use of a recognized right does not allow another solution than the legality of the act, even though it may cause a harm. As the doctrine uses to recall, the acts practiced by the creditor in the enforced execution of the obligation (ex vi, protest, attachment, arrestment, bid) are harmful to the debtor, but they do not cast the right of civil compensation, thus are licit acts. The exigence required is that the due exercise of rights is done in a "regular" manner to delineate the border with the situation of abuse. As recalls Theodoro Junior:[239]

> Being at stake the ethical values, it is hard to the legislator to translate them, hypothetically, in positive norms. It will always fall under the prudent criteria of the judge, regarding the circumstances of the concrete case, to identify where, really, is located the due use of a right and where lies its abusive exercise. It is in this field that is imperious the reasonable logic and not the pure logic.
>
> As adverts Pereira, the individual, in acting in its right, "must contain himself in the realm of reasonability." If this limit is trespassed, on who exercises faculties that are technically in his right, and provokes an unnecessary or unjust evil, that agent "even his behavior to the illicit, and, instead of liability's exemption, it will incur in compensatory duty."
>
> The exercise of one's own right cannot be done to violate the rights of another. The rights of every person ends where the others begin. In every conflict of rights – which have only a shade of conflict – the legal order and its general criteria to define whose interests must prevail and whose interests are meant to be cast aside. Therefore, the abusive exercise occurs, exactly, when the right's owner prevails himself of it to harm a third party who has the right to oppose to him, to avoid the harm the first wants to inflict to him.
>
> "In true, there is no right against right; and it is absurd that the exercise an own right could conduce to the violation of another's right, as the law cannot protect at the same time the interests of the harmed and the agent of the harm."
>
> "Which is why, by exercising irregularly his right to cause harm to another, who legally does not have the obligation to support the excess performed, the right's owner exits the licit realm and enters in the illicit one (Art. 187)."

III. Self-Defense

177. There is no concept of "self-defense" in the Civil Code, reason that the doctrine uses to employ a definition presented in the Article 25 of the Brazilian Criminal Code ("it can be understood as in self-defense one, who using the moderate necessary means, dispel unjust aggression, current or imminent to his/her or

239. *Ibid.*

another's right"). Noronha summoned Dias to say, "the self-defense is a qualified necessity state."[240] As affirms Theodoro Junior:[241]

> ... the Civil Code states that 'does not constitute illicit acts those practiced in self-defense (Art. 188, I). Does not care the civil rules, about configuring it through the description of its elements or requisites. Therefore, it is in the criminal law that the private applier will find the means to concept the illicit exemption clause that is in here treated. Firstly, it is extracted from the criminal concept that the self-defense victim can be used to dispel the aggression to his/her own as for other goods. In addition, it is established the following requisites catalogued by the Criminal Code (Art. 21), to be demonstrated so the harm agent beneficiates himself/herself from the exemption clause of self-defense: a) current or imminent and unjust aggression; b) preservation of a right from his/her own or from another; c) use of moderated means necessary to defense. It is not considered as self-defense the preemptive aggression against future harms that are remotely predictable. It is necessary that the reaction is given against current or imminent evil, from a manner that the aggressed was not able to defend oneself in other fashion that not the immediate use of force to preserve oneself of his goods. One must act, though, in the strictly necessary fashion to dispel the harm that threatens him/her. It could not, after the aggression be dismissed to pass to retaliation or vendetta. The excessive defense is off-limits to the licit field and makes it an abuse of rights, configuring illicit act beyond of the necessary to dispel the unjust aggression (Art. 187).

§3. Exemption from Causation

178. In some occasions, someone whom is liable for a harmful fact can demonstrate that the harm, effectively is not connected to him/her by the act practiced (partially or entirely), and actually for another fact, binding other agent, and therefore exempting (or "interrupting") the causation nexus. It dispels the incidence of a determined cause for the determination of the existence of another, usually more relevant, from which origins the exclusion of civil liability regarding one of the authors.[242]

I. Victim's Exclusive Fact

179. The victims' exclusive fact occurs when the acts of the harmful agents are not relevant to the configuration of the harm itself, as the victim's own acts are. In the definition of Noronha,[243] "as the expression. Indicates, the harmed fact, also

240. See NORONHA, Direito das Obrigações, 2010, São Paulo, at 375.
241. See THEODORO JUNIOR, Comentários ao Novo Código Civil, 2003, Rio de Janeiro, at 137.
242. See CRUZ, O Problema do Nexo Causal na Responsabilidade Civil, 2005, Rio de Janeiro, at 155.
243. See NORONHA, Direito das Obrigações, 2010, São Paulo, at 620.

known as victim's fact, is the one attributed to the act of the own person who suffered the harm. When the actuation of the harmed is from his/her own, there is no reason to talk about paying damages (except in special occasions of great strict liability) … ." The victim's act, in this case, does not limits to concur (contribute) to the harm (hypothesis that will be analyzed next), but is exclusive causation to the harmful fact, from which the imputation to another agent lies unjustified.

II. Third Party's Act

180. In the same rational, the third party's acts are connected to the relevance of another's acts as opposed to the main agent appointed to be liable for the harm and the victim itself, as states Noronha:[244] the third party's fact is a causation excluding (and therefore, usually also an exemption clause) is the anti-juridical act practiced by one who is not the harmed or the possible whose liability is being analyzed... The third party's act cannot be an excluding of liability in the great strict liability cases. On the other hand, it may be the very determinant to the other's liability, when the harm is caused by a person, independently of the one who was firstly attributed as the agent; in these cases, it can be considered as liability for the fact of other.

III. Fortuity and Act of God

181. The Fortuity and the Act of God are situations where no sole human can resist, being connected to the natural or collective human phenomenon. As states Noronha:[245]

> When the expressions Fortuity or Act of God are used in the strict sense (and without distinguishing fortuity from the act of god) it encompasses natural facts such as storms, floods and diseases (which can be named acts of God), and human actions, not individualized, such as war, robbery, depredations, and even authority demonstrations, always that such facts are determinant to the harm caused. The imposition of an authority that have generated a harm, its traditionally called factum principis. The human actions that are not individualized that, along with nature facts are related to fortuity and act of god in the strict sense, many times are close to third party's acts. Therefore, for instance, if the third party's act will be the reason to the loss of goods transported by a truck, when resulted by accident of other truck, when the other is out of control as could be considered as fortuity or act of god the same loss, when the goods were stolen in an assault with guns headed by a gang.

244. See NORONHA, Direito das Obrigações, 2010, São Paulo, at 620.
245. See NORONHA, Direito das Obrigações, 2010, São Paulo, at 621.

IV. Contributory Causation

182. The situation of co-causality in which is identified the participation of different agents that may result in joint liability (in case of co-authors, as states the paragraph of the Article 942 of the Civil Code), or liability's mitigation (case described in the Article 945 of the same code). Even though the reference to "fault" in the Article 945, it actually is about the causation contribution of the harmed to the occurrence of the harm itself, as well refers Cruz,[246] through the connection to Dias. As observes Lisboa,[247] demonstrated the participation of the harmed in the occurrence (or in the dimension) of the harm, there are three possible solutions ("the proportional division of suffered losses," "the proportionality of fault of each co-authors" and "the degree of participation of each in the causation to the result"), "the causation principle must prevail, to ends of determination of the harm compensation." The system adopted by the Brazilian Law is very close to the da comparative negligence of Common Law.[248] It is not about exactly the "causation dismiss" (and, therefore, the "exclusion of civil liability") but, more precisely, of realizing the presence of another cause, with the mitigation of the responsible agent (through the application of the proportionality rule), due the conclusion that the harm only acquired its total dimension by the joint collaboration between agent and victim.

§4. Statutory Limitations

183. According to the Article 206, §3, V, of the Brazilian Civil Code, it is limited in three years the "pretension of civil compensation." In consumption relations, in the terms of the Article 27 of Lei nº 8.078/90 ("Consumer's Defense Code"), "is limited in five years the reparation by harms caused for products or services fact." The statutory limitations, in any case, despite it does not extinguished the right to compensation (if there is a compliance to it by the harm's agent it will be the due fulfillment to the obligation), it will deter the possibility for the harmed to demand the reparation in judicial and extrajudicial procedures.

246. See CRUZ, O Problema do Nexo Causal na Responsabilidade Civil, 2005, Rio de Janeiro, at 343.
247. See LISBOA, Manual de Direito Civil, vol. 2 – Obrigações e Responsabilidade Civil, 2004, São Paulo, at 521.
248. In the contrary that the expression "contributory causation" or "contributory fault" may suggest, in Common Law the concurrent negligence is more adequate to the situation of complementary causation discussed in Part IV.

Part V. Causation

184. There is not, in Brazilian Law, a specific rule about causation in the Torts System. However, the doctrine[249] and jurisprudence[250] recognize its content in Article 403 of the Civil Code (which give the rules for loss and harms) the fundament for the recognition of a criteria for the causation. In this article is written that "even that the inexecution results from the debtor's intent, the loss and harms will only include the effective harms and the profit loss for its immediate and direct effect." Even though seems evident that this rule is directed to the contractual liability, (the expression "inexecution" indicate this specificity), and the lack of any other indication of that theme in the positive law anchors the theme to this article.

185. As it's known, the first theories about causation emerged in the Continental Law, are derivations of the Philosophic conceptions about the subject and, in this sense, had as a starting point the idea of "physics" or "mechanics," or even, "naturalist" of causation. As assigns Hart and Honoré,[251] the expression is a modern to the notion *versari in re illicita* as exposed by Glaser (1858), in Austria, and right after by von Buri, in Germany (1860), with the idea that any necessary condition or sine qua non of an event is its causation. The emerging of the *Bedingungstheorie*, or condition's theory or equivalence of condition's theory. According to this starting point, it is possible to perceive the adequate causation as an essay of sophistication, in order to precise the notion of cause, though still in an objective and naturalistic idea. The same can be affirmed to the variants of the adequate causation, as the direct harm (and immediate).

186. In another line is positioned the norm protection theory, that identifies the notion of cause in the normative element (axiological), depriving it from any naturalistic bound and approximating it to the attribution factor. As it was stated, the condition's equivalency theory does not distinguish causation and condition: if, any conditions concur for the same result, every one of them have the same value (all of them are equal). Therefore, in order to know if determined condition is the cause, it will be mentally excluded for a hypothetical process: if the result disappears, the condition is the causation. In the evolution of this theory is found the adequate causality, which individualizes or qualifies the condition. Cause is the antecedent that is not only necessary, but also adequate to the production of the result. Therefore,

249. See CRUZ, O Problema do Nexo Causal na Responsabilidade Civil, 2005, Rio de Janeiro, at 97.
250. STJ. REsp 1557978/DF, 03/11/15. Brasilia.
251. See HART and HONORÉ, Causation in The Law, 1959, Oxford, at 442–443.

not every condition is cause to the fact, only these conditions that are more appropriated to produce the event. Following the same authors (p. 466), von Bar was the precursor (1870) of what is called the "generalization school" (thus, these authors are "generic" the theories that every individual causation if implicitly general, in the sense that its veracity depends only on a general affirmation about its empiric regularities), taking as a starting point the work of Glaser, though, contesting his conclusion that any condition must be considered as a cause. For von Bar, any cause is necessarily a condition, but not any condition is a cause, thus this quality can be only given to these events that are aside the "regularity" ("regular" events or "ordinary," therefore, even if they are conditions, they are not causes). This theory was later developed by von Kries (1880), that incorporated elements of probabilistic analysis in the notion of "regularity of events" proposed by von Bar.[252] According to Noronha,[253] the theory admits a "positive" formulation ("a fact must be considered an adequate cause of a posterior event when it favors the production of it") and "negative" ("adequate Is the cause that, following the experience rules, is not indifferent to the emergence of the harm"), considering as preferable the second. It is sustained as applicable in the Brazilian Law ordainment.[254]

187. A variant of the last theory is the "direct harm," affirmed in Brazil by Alvim, thus "the cause of a harm can be a close or remote fact, but it must be directed connected to it." In the Supreme Federal Court (Supremo Tribunal Federal), by the occasion of the RE 130764/PR, trial, the Rapporteur, Minister Moreira Alves, affirmed that this theory funds the causation in the Brazilian Civil Law. It is also the position of, among others, Gonçalves.[255] Cruz[256] details that the Brazilian doctrine's perspective about this theory. Other variants of adequate causation are the "efficient causation" and the "preponderant causation."[257] In the direction of a rupture with the "naturalistic" idea of cause, though recognizing the existence of a protection of the norm ambit, (or "harm to the protected good"), which states that is not possible to identify a sole criterion to define the causation in every hypothesis of civil liability, but to observe the violated norm's function.[258] Finally, and in a strictly normative perspective, are the theories that states the strict imputation of causation (encompassing, therefore, the attribution factor and the causation nexus), with no notable influence in Brazil.[259]

188. It is Worth of mention, in the causation doctrine, in civil liability, the theme of multiple causes, which can be presented in many forms. As a rule, the condition sine qua non, criteria or the necessary condition, is accepted in the private law

252. See SANTOLIM, Nexo de Causalidade e Prevenção na Responsabilidade Civil, Revista da AJURIS – v. 41 – n. 136 – December 2014, Porto Alegre.
253. See NORONHA, Direito das Obrigações, 2010, São Paulo, at 601–602.
254. *Ibid.*, at 603.
255. See GONÇALVES, Direito Civil Brasileiro, 2007, São Paulo, at 333–334.
256. See CRUZ, O Problema do Nexo Causal na Responsabilidade Civil, 2005, Rio de Janeiro, at 107.
257. For a deeper comprehension of the theories, see CRUZ, *supra*, 2005.
258. See SANTOLIM, Nexo de Causalidade e Prevenção na Responsabilidade Civil, Revista da AJURIS – v. 41 – n. 136 – December 2014, Porto Alegre.
259. See CRUZ, O Problema do Nexo Causal na Responsabilidade Civil, 2005, Rio de Janeiro, at 122.

doctrine, as a minimum necessary for the causation, which would give the maximum notion of causation, though this procedure would conduct to odd results in cases of multiple causes. It is what happens in hypothesis of cumulative causations, in which the result would be equally produced without the cause, and thus, this was not a necessary condition.

189. Other problem considered as relevant to the subject, it of the "virtual causation" or "hypothetic causation" (fact given as adequate to the production of the result, though is not enough to produce it, due another fact, that alters the causation chain) that would generates what Noronha[260] details as interrupted causation (when the real causa is invoked by the author of the virtual cause – positive relevance of the virtual cause) or anticipated causation (when the author of the real cause is the one who alleges the existence of a virtual cause – negative relevance of the virtual cause). In a general sense, it is denied a legal relevance to the "virtual cause," even though they exist, as affirms the author "situations more complex," from which can be highlighted the mitigation of the damages values.

190. Also known as "complementary causation," which happens when "both actions would only cause the harm together, being the complementarity of the causes necessary (e.g., two doses of venom, which by themselves are not lethal are disposed in a coffee by two different persons and together they provoke a person's death),"[261] is worthy of consideration in Brazilian Law.[262] The causes can be presented in simultaneous or successive ways, in any case, there is not a problem of "super determination of causation" facing the dispositions of the paragraph of Article 942 of the Brazilian Civil Code ("are liable in solidarity the authors with the co-authors").

191. Though in not necessary cumulative causation,[263] "each action was by itself a cause, which is enough to cause the harmful event (for instance, two mortal doses of poison dropped in the same coffee by two different persons...)."[264] In this context, earns importance the distinction mentioned by Acciarri,[265] between conditions NESS (necessary element of a sufficient set) and INUS (insufficient but non-redundant part of an unnecessary but sufficient condition). By, adopting the first criteria, as mentioned by Hart and Honoré,[266] in cases of super determination of causation, each necessary element of these bundles are "eligible" as a cause.

---

260. See NORONHA, Direito das Obrigações, 2010, São Paulo, at 658.
261. See PINTO, Sobre Condição e Causa na Responsabilidade Civil, 2008, Coimbra, at 933.
262. See LISBOA, Manual de Direito Civil, vol. 2 – Obrigações e Responsabilidade Civil, 2004, São Paulo, at 518.
263. The expression was coined by PINTO, at 933.
264. See ACCIARRI, La Relación de Causalidad y las Funciones del Derecho de Daños, 2009, Buenos Aires, at 22. According to the author, the terms were coined by J.L. Mackie.
265. *Supra*, at 112.
266. Critiques of the use of NESS and their refutations can be found in WRIGHT, The NESS Account of Natural Causation: A Response to Criticisms. Available at <http://scholarship.kentlaw.iit.edu/fac_schol/716>. Published: Jan. 1, 2011. Accessed on May 12, 2014. In this work, Wright distinguishes the NESS criteria of the two others attributed to Hart and Honoré ("factor with causality relevance") and John Mackie (conditions INUS).

192. The Brazilian doctrine[267] recognizes, in addition, the alternative causation in which exists "uncertainty about what was, of the diversity of causes, the one which has produced the result."[268] Alternatively, in the description of Noronha,[269] "when there are two or more facts with potentialities to cause a determined harm, but is not known which one is the true cause."

267. See LISBOA, Manual de Direito Civil, vol. 2 – Obrigações e Responsabilidade Civil, 2004, São Paulo, at 518.
268. See PINTO, Sobre Condição e Causa na Responsabilidade Civil, 2008, Coimbra, at 933.
269. See NORONHA, Direito das Obrigações, 2010, São Paulo, at 652.

Part VI. Remedies

Chapter 1. General Principles

193. The harm is an element or essential requisite, condition sine qua non to the Civil Liability. Resulting the Torts System in the obligation to pay damages, and therefore, logically it cannot be fulfilled where there is nothing to repair. The notion of harm supposes that the victim has been harmed from a situation from his/her fruition, being damaged in a former advantage. Therefore, in the legal realm, in essence, the notion of harm is related to the damage caused to the victim, the subtraction of value or good from the victim.[270] In the formal definition of Cavalieri Filho: "the harm is the subtraction of diminishing of a legal good, whatever its nature, either from a patrimonial good, or a part of the own personality of the victim, as its honor, image, liberty, etc … ."[271]

194. The economic notion of damage is analogous to the legal notion. As Cooter and Ulen register, "Harm has a simple economic interpretation: a downward shift in the victim's utility or profit function," being the goal of damages, the restitution of the integrity of the victim.[272] It can be inferred, then, under the legal perspective or under the economic one, the basic idea inherent to the harm element is bounded to the damage, to the reparation or compensation, so the victim can return to the situation before the harm or so the victim can be compensated for the modification of his/her status before the harm. In other words, the basic idea, inherent to the element harm is bounded to the victim damages to correct the external defects of the acts practiced by the author – negative externalities.[273]

195. The reparation of harms, the correction of external effects of the act practiced by the author, can be specific, as the reconstruction of the situation of a fact prior to the harm, or can be equivalent, through the delivery of pecuniary values to the victim. Though the obligation to pay damages can be fulfilled through the reposition of things from the debtor to the condition prior to the harmful event (natural reparation or *in natura*), its more recurrent that the damages take the form of a pecuniary nature, to be fulfilled with the delivery to the creditor of money correspondent

270. See DIAS, Da Responsabilidade Civil, Rio de Janeiro, 2006, at 969, and Pereira, Responsabilidade Civil, 2012. Rio de Janeiro, at 54–56.
271. See CAVALIERI FILHO, Programa de Responsabilidade Civil, 2012, São Paulo, at 73.
272. See COOTER & ULEN, Law and Economics, 2008, Boston, at 326 and 389.
273. See BATTESINI, Direito e Economia, Novos Horizontes no Estudo da Responsabilidade Civil no Brasil, 2011, São Paulo, at 250.

to compensation for the patrimonial and extra-patrimonial losses suffered.[274] In practice, the attribution of responsibility for harms supposes that the harms can be evaluated and calculated, which, by its turn, supposes that it is possible to isolate the harms and attribute a monetary value to them or to restitute the victim to the prior status quo. In cases in which it is not possible to determine a monetary amount that let the victim indifferent between a world with the losses and a world without the losses (as, for example, great injuries, death, etc., the solution is to determine a monetary value which can, at least bring some additional utility to the victim.[275]

196. The association of the compensation idea, the reestablishment or reconstruction to a prior situation, that would be, if the harmful event were not, the pecuniary character of damages, has its corollary in the classic legal rule of the monetary correspondence between the damages and the harm, of the proportionality or symmetry between the damages and the harm. Symmetry which is crystallized by the Civil Liability doctrine, and can be found in the Brazilian system in the caput of Article 944 of the Brazilian Civil Code of 2002, which expressively established that "the damages are measured by the extension of the harm."[276]

197. In the systematics of the Brazilian Civil Code of 2002, the civil liability (title IX) is regulated in two chapters. In Chapter 1, the Code established the necessary elements to characterize the duty to pay damages, encompassing a general clause of reparation of harms in the Article 927, "one that, by illicit act, cause harms to other, is obliged to repair it." In Chapter 2, the Code treats the theme of damages, establishing the general principles of harms liquidation in Articles 944–947. In addition, in Articles 944–947, the Code regulates the specific aspects related to the damages in specific cases as homicide (Articles 948 and 951); injuries or offenses to health (Articles 949, 950 and 951); usurpation or divestment of another's property (Article 952); injury, defamation, or calumny (Article 953), and; offenses to the personal liberty (Article 954). It must be highlighted, in addition, that the Brazilian judiciary has developed and important role in the definition of the reparable harms and the fixation of paying damages obligation criteria.

274. See ANDRADE, Dano Moral e Indenização Punitiva: Os Punitive Damages na Experiência da Common Law e na Perspectiva do Direito Brasileiro, 2009, Rio de Janeiro, at 141, and COELHO, Curso de Direito Civil, Responsabilidade Civil, 2005, São Paulo, at 397–398.

275. See SCHAEFFER, Hand-Bernd and Klaus, OTT, The Economic Analysis of Civil Law, 2004, Cheltenham, at 131 and 247.

276. See BATTESINI, Direito e Economia, Novos Horizontes no Estudo da Responsabilidade Civil no Brasil, 2011, São Paulo, at 251.

Chapter 2. Kinds of Damages

§1. Individual and Collective Damage

198. Even though the Brazilian Civil Code of 2002 does not make any differentiation between individual and collective damages, these categories are present in the Brazilian system of Torts, either by specific legislation or by doctrinaire and jurisprudential construction. The Brazilian doctrine refers to the individual harms as those that may affect determined people's integrity, physical, psychical, or moral, or in the things, which composes their patrimony. The collective harms, also denominated trans-individual or supra individual are those that tackle goods of a generic number of people that are integrated in a collective.[277]

199. The preoccupation with collective goods is one of the characteristics of the contemporary evolution of the Brazilian system of torts.[278] The Lei nº 4.717, of June 29, 1965, disciplines the popular class action, that legitimize any citizen to ask for annulations or declaration of nullities of acts harming the Union, the Federal District, the States of Municipalities patrimony, as the respective members of the indirect administration specified in the legal text. The Lei nº 7.347, of July 24th, 1985, disciplines the civil class action for environment, consumer, goods and values of artistic nature, aesthetic, historical, touristic and landscape harms, attributing in its Article 5, legitimacy to the proposition of the legal suit to the Public Ministry, the Public Defender, the Union, the Federal District, the States, the Municipalities, the Autarchies, Public Firms, Foundations, Societies of Mixed Economy, and Associations that filled the special requirements of the legal text. The object of condemnations in civil class actions, according to the Article 3 of the legal text, can consist in payment of damages, obligations of doing, or not to do, being the damages applicable only when the reparation *in natura* is not an option. The theme of the collective moral harms has leveled controversies in the jurisprudential plane. The First Group of the Superior Court of Justice (Superior Tribunal de Justiça) has denied the application of collective moral harms based on the impossibility to determine the passive subject, indivisibility of the offense and therefore, the reparation.[279] On the other hand, the 2nd Group of the same court has admitted the collective moral harm configuration.[280]

277. See NORONHA, Direito das Obrigações, 2010, São Paulo, at 596.

278. See SCHREIBER, Novos Paradigmas da Responsabilidade Civil, 2009, São Paulo, at 84–85, and NADER, Curso de Direito Civil, Responsabilidade Civil, 2014, Rio de Janeiro, at 81–82.

279. STJ, 1ª Turma, REsp 598.281/MG, Relator Ministro Luiz Fux, DJ. 01.06.2006, p. 147. Brasília.

280. STJ, 2ª Turma, REsp 1.057.274/RS, Relatora Ministra Eliana Calmon, DJe. 26.02.2010. Brasília.

§2. Direct and Indirect

200. The Brazilian system of torts admits the reparation of harms caused directly to the victim, which are in the immediate effect of the harmful fact, and the reparation of harms caused indirectly to the victims, which, not being affected immediately, have connection to the harmful fact.[281] A special category of indirect harms are the reflex harms or ricochet, in which the harmful fact, in addition to the direct victim, harms a third party that was also harmed by his/her connection to the victim in the harmful fact, as the son that fails to receive nourishment by virtue of the death of his/her father in an accident. As occurs with the direct harms, the indirect harms may be defined and certain or hypothetical or eventual.[282]

201. Under influence of the civilian French doctrine, the Brazilian jurisprudence has chosen the theory of a chance's loss (*perte d'une chance*), a complex theme that, in a nutshell, admits the reparation of a harm caused by a harmful fact that determines the suppression of a possibility of event that may proportionate a better future or to avoid a future loss to the victim. The loss of a chance, usually, constitutes an indirect harm in which the author's liability depends of the configuration of the causation and the loss of a real chance and not a remote probability.[283] The loss of a chance theory has been recognized by the Superior Court of Justice (Superior Tribunal de Justiça), being applied by the jurisprudence in situations such as: loss of a chance to an adequate medical treatment, caused by delay in the diagnosis of a pathology,[284] and; loss of a chance to obtain a favorable legal decision, due a deadline loss caused by the attorney.[285]

§3. Pecuniary and Non-pecuniary Losses

202. A distinction between material, also known as patrimonial or pecuniary, and moral harms, also known as extra-patrimonial or non-pecuniary, has as a starting point the concept of patrimony, comprehended as a bundle of goods of a person that as susceptible to economic evaluation, in pecuniary terms. Therefore, in the doctrinaire realm, it is understood that the material harms are the ones that occurs from violation of interests bounded to the patrimony of the victim, of economic concrete interests, directly susceptible to pecuniary evaluation. On the other hand, the moral harms are the ones that occur by the violation of non-patrimonial interests of

281. See NORONHA, Direito das Obrigações, 2010, São Paulo, at 602–603.
282. See NADER, Curso de Direito Civil, Responsabilidade Civil, 2014, Rio de Janeiro, at 79–80.
283. See CAVALIERI FILHO, Programa de Responsabilidade Civil, 2012, São Paulo, at 77–81, and PEREIRA, Responsabilidade Civil, Rio de Janeiro, 2012, at 60–62.
284. STJ, 3ª Turma, REsp 1.335.622/DF, Relator Ministro Ricardo Villas Bôas Cueva, DJe. 27.02.2013. Brasília.
285. STJ, 4ª Turma, REsp 1.190.180/RS, Relator Ministro Luis Felipe Salomão, DJe. 22.11.2010. Brasília.

the victim, or the ones that can be translated into a violation of interests not susceptible to pecuniary evaluation.[286]

203. The 2002's Brazilian Civil Code does not define the material and moral harms, as does not delimitates what would be the harms to be defended by the rule of law. Even though, the Brazilian system of torts reaches expressively both harms modalities, referring to them in the Article 5, V and X, and in the Article 114, VI, both from the Federal Constitution of 1988, as in the Article 186 of the Civil code of 2002, as the moral harms as opposed to the material harms.[287]

204. The material harms, encompasses the wide branch of corporeal and non-corporeal things that composes the patrimony of the victim, such as the house, the vehicle, books, credit rights, etc... The moral harms, by their turn, are related to the personality rights, such as the name, the honor, the liberty, the physical integrity, the image, the intimacy and the private life.[288] In practical terms, in the absence of objective criteria established in law, relevant role in the configuration of what is or is not moral harm is attributed to the doctrine and jurisprudence.

205. In the doctrinaire realm, it is paradigmatic the manifestation of Cavalieri Filho[289] in the sense that in the characterization of moral harms are necessary the observation of "rules of good prudence, in the practical sense, of the just measure of things, of a complete ponderation of the realities of life." The author follows his comprehension that:

> In this line of principal, it can only be reputed as moral the pain, the harassment, suffering of humiliation that, escaping the normality, interferes intensely in the psychological behavior of the individual, causing to him/her afflictions, angst and disequilibria in its well-being. A mere dislike, disturbances, upsetting, irritation or high sensibility are out of the scope of the moral harm, thus, aside being part of our daily life's normality in work, traffic and between friends and even among the familiar environment, these situations are not as intense and lasting to break the psychological equilibria of the individual.

206. The jurisprudence identifies a wide spectrum of situations in which the moral harms are characterizes, referring to: the unauthorized use of photographic or cinematographic images;[290] the injuries to the physical integrity occurrence such as sight loss, amputation of members, the irreversible state of coma, aesthetic

286. See NORONHA, Direito das Obrigações, 2010, São Paulo, at 590, and DINIZ, Curso de Direito Civil Brasileiro, Responsabilidade Civil, 2009, São Paulo, at 67–68 and 90–91.
287. See FARIAS, BRAGA NETTO & ROSENVALD, Novo Tratado de Responsabilidade Civil, 2015, São Paulo, at 229, and NORONHA, Direito das Obrigações, 2010, São Paulo, at 590.
288. See NADER, Curso de Direito Civil, Responsabilidade Civil, 2014. Rio de Janeiro, at 84–87, and NORONHA, Direito das Obrigações, 2010, São Paulo, at 593.
289. See CAVALIERI FILHO, Programa de Responsabilidade Civil, 2012, São Paulo, at 86–87.
290. STJ, 3ª Turma, REsp 1.323.586/PB, Relator Ministro Ricardo Villas Bôas Cueva, DJe. 11.03.2015; STJ, 2ª Turma, REsp 1.289.679/RS, Relatora Ministra Eliana Calmon, DJe. 18.09.2013. Brasilia.

deformities, contamination by HIV in blood transfusion;[291] the occurrence of injuries to the intimacy and private life by the press for legally protected facts;[292] the erratic inscription of legal or natural persons in the debtors list;[293] the erratic protest in commercial title;[294] the publishing of calumnious or untruthful line by the press;[295] delays in the expedition of university diploma;[296] lack of assistance to passenger in flight delayed after four hours;[297] the erratic imprisonment by legal mistake.[298] The Superior Court of Justice (Superior Tribunal de Justiça) has pacified the comprehension that are computable both material and moral harms damages, even if they are related to the same fact.[299]

§4. Pure Economic Loss

207. In Brazilian legal system, pure economic loss generally is recoverable under the rules of contract law. Tort law does not generally allow compensation for pure economic loss. Pure economic interests are protected as such only by certain provisions, as is the case of the Article 950 of the Brazilian Civil Code of 2002:

> if from the offense results defects by which the offended cannot exercise its job or profession, if it is diminished his/her work capacity, the damage, in addition to the expenses of the treatment and ceased profits until the end of convalescence, will include pension correspondent to the importance of the work for he/her was disabled or to the depreciation suffered.

In environmental matters, with fundament in the Article 14, paragraph 1, of lei nº 6.938/81, is admitted the reparation of pure economic losses caused to third parties, as for example, with the payment of damages by restrictions to the fishing activities through the emission of contaminants such as oil and mining effluents in river and sea waters.[300]

291. STJ, 2ª Turma, REsp 1.363.881/MG, Relator Ministro Herman Benjamin, DJe. 03.07.2014; STJ, 4ª Turma, REsp 1.248.206/SP, Relator Ministro Marco Buzzi, DJe. 20.08.2015; STJ, 3ª Turma, REsp 1.349.968/DF, Relator Ministro Marco Aurélio Bellizze, DJe. 14.04.2015; STJ, 4ª Turma, REsp 655.761/SP, Relator Ministro Marco Buzzi, DJe. 03.02.2015. Brasilia.
292. STJ, 3ª Turma, REsp 1.380701/PA, Relator Ministro Marco Aurélio Bellizze, DJe. 14.05.2015. Brasilia.
293. STJ, 4ª Turma, REsp 655.761/SP, Relator Ministro Marco Buzzi, DJe. 03.02.2015. Brasília.
294. STJ, 3ª Turma, REsp 1.434.508/BA, Relator Ministro Sidnei Beneti, DJe. 04.06.2014. Brasília.
295. STJ, 4ª Turma, REsp 1.365.284/SC, Luis Felipe Salomão, DJe. 21.10.2014. Brasília.
296. STJ, 2ª Turma, REsp 1.524.143/PR, Relator Ministro Herman Benjamin, DJe. 30.06.2015. Brasília.
297. STJ, 3ª Turma, REsp 1.280.372/SP, Relator Ministro Ricardo Villas Bôas Cueva, DJe. 10.10.2014. Brasília.
298. STJ, 2ª Turma, REsp 1.385.946/MG, Relator Ministro Herman Benjamin, DJe. 15.04.2014. Brasilia.
299. STJ, súmula nº 37. Brasilia.
300. STJ, 2ª Seção, REsp 1.145.358/PR, Relator Ministro Ricardo Villas Bôas Cueva, DJe. 09.05.2012. Brasilia.

§5. Actual and Future Damage (Lost Profits)

208. Adopting as reference determined temporal mark, such as the legal decision that determined the reparation, harms can be classified as present or current and future. Have present harms occurred effectively, are these verified by the moment they are evaluated.[301] Briefly, the difference between current and future harms is present in the Brazilian system of torts. In the terms of Article 402 of the Brazilian civil code, "the pecuniary losses due to the creditor encompass, in addition to what he/she effectively lost, what he/she reasonably has ceased to profit." The effective losses of the victim, the diminishing in its patrimony by the harmful fact, constitutes the emergent harms, for example, the material harms verify in a vehicle in a traffic accident. What the victim reasonably has ceased to profit, the gains that, following the natural order of things, probably would flow to the patrimony of the victim if the harmful fact was not, constitutes the ceasing profits, for instance, the stopping of earnings of a doctor, that, due an accident is incapable to exercise his/her profession for a determined period of time.[302]

§6. Other Costs

209. In the terms of the Brazilian Civil Procedure Code of 2015,[303] it is due to the defeated party in legal right to pay for the procedural expenses, such as the acts practiced in the procedure and the payment to the expert (Article 82, §2°, along with the Article 84), in addition to the payment of attorney fees to the winner party (Article 85). In a nutshell, the attorney fees are given by the judge in observation to the minimum percent of ten a maximum of 20% of the value of condemnation, of the economic profit or the current value of the cause (Article 85, §2°). Differential treatment is assigned to the State observing the minimum percentage of one and a maximum of 20% of the value of the conviction or economic advantage. In civil liability suits for illicit against persons, the fee's will be applied upon the sum of the due quotes added by twelve future quotes (Article 85, §9°). In case of reciprocal loss, the procedural expenses and attorney fees are proportionally distributed between the parties (Article 86).

§7. Mitigation of Damages

210. The topic of mitigation of damages is not object of legal prediction in the Brazilian legal system. Even though, in some sense, the mitigation of damages is

301. See FARIAS, BRAGA NETTO and ROSENVALD, Novo Tratado de Responsabilidade Civil, 2015, São Paulo, at 275, and Noronha, Direito das Obrigações, São Paulo, 2010, at 603.
302. See GONÇALVES, Responsabilidade Civil, 2006, São Paulo, at 652–653, and CAVALIERI FILHO, Programa de Responsabilidade Civil, 2012, São Paulo, at 74–75.
303. Law n° 13.105, of Mar. 16, 2015. Código de Processo Civil.

considered an aspect of the injured party's contributory fault. In the terms of the Article 945 of the Civil Code, "if the victim has concurred faulty to the harmful event, the damages will be given according to the extension of its fault facing the harm's author own fault."

Chapter 3. Assessment and Compensation of Damages

§1. Objective versus Subjective

211. Briefly, the assessment and compensation of damages is done considering the value that the object would have for anybody. The value is determined by an objective method, usually by the market price. However, the specific value that the object has for the victim is considered by Brazilian system of tort in specific situations, as is the case of usurpation or divestment of the thing. According to the paragraph of the Article 952 of the Civil Code, "in order to restitute the equivalent, when does not exist the thing itself, it will be estimated by its ordinary price and approximation, given that the last does not overcome the first." There is, therefore, that the Brazilian legislator, nevertheless admits the weight of subjective values of the victim in the case of usurpation or dispossession of the thing, establishes an objective limitation, namely that the amount of compensation to be fixed by the emotional loss cannot be arbitrated in an amount higher than the market value of the thing.[304]

§2. Concrete versus Abstract

212. Concerning the assessment and compensation of harms in Brazilian system of tort law, the distinction between concrete and abstract is usually not done. As a rule, the evaluation and compensation of harms must be done in a concrete way. The term abstract is rarely used, but, anyway, could be suitable in the cases of loss of a chance and loss of profits, in which the profits could have been expected with probability according to the particular circumstances or the ordinary course of the events.

§3. Methods of Assessing Damages

213. In the Brazilian system of torts, the basic criteria or the value determination is given by the caput of Article 944 of the Civil Code, which is "the damage is given by the extension of the harm." It is, in essence, the positivation of the *restitutio in integrum* principle, representing the ideal to seek, as possible, the relocation of the victim in the situation prior to the harm suffered. The criteria of the extension of harm is objective, and must orientate the judicial actuation regarding the kind and portion to be paid by the debtor, in order to reestablish the anti-legal misconduct's broken equilibria.[305]

304. See GONÇALVES, Responsabilidade Civil, 2006, São Paulo, at 728–729, and NADER, Curso de Direito Civil, Responsabilidade Civil, 2014, Rio de Janeiro, at 221.
305. See GAMA, in: RODRIGUES JUNIOR, MAMEDE e ROCHA, Responsabilidade Civil Contemporânea, 2011, São Paulo, at 600–602.

214. Regarding the material damages, it is widely diffused the difference theory, by which the due value is given by the difference of the current value of the victim's patrimony and the value of the victim's patrimony if the harm was not. Which is, if the harm correspondent to a patrimonial value given by the difference, considering the time of the harmful event and the time of the victim compensation.[306] As a rule, the determination of the loss of patrimonial value is given considering the Market value of the goods considered.

215. As for the moral harms, they obey the principle of the compensatory satisfaction, according to the sum of pecuniary compensation to be due to the victim cannot assume a character of "price," but a compensatory character to the suffering, physical or psychological pain, inflicted to the victim from the harm to its personality rights. Differently from the rules of material or patrimony harms, in which the market gives objective data to the determination of the damages, in the case of extra-patrimonial harms, the fixation of damages depends essentially of the equitable evaluation of the judiciary.[307] In the pecuniary quantification of the compensation to moral harms, the judiciary has considered standards such as: the economic level of the author and the victim, the degree of fault of the author and the victim, the greatness of the harm, the circumstances of the event, the impact of the harm under the victim and the social repercussion of the event.[308] The control of the value of the damages competes to the Superior Court of Justice (Superior Tribunal de Justiça),[309] which has acted as "Libra" in the ponderation to the interests involved, making the balance of damages values in a bundle of representative cases, such as: death of Family members, erratic inscription in debtor's lists, erratic line published in press, illegal imprisonment, and unjustified flight cancelation.[310]

§4. Equitable Limitation of Damages

216. The equitable limitation of damages in relation to the harm is admitted in the Brazilian system of Torts, adopting as a basic criterion de fault's degree of the author and of the victim.[311] In addition to the basic rule of the symmetry between the damage and the harm predicted in the caput of the Article 944, "the damage is

306. See NADER, Curso de Direito Civil, Responsabilidade Civil, 2014, Rio de Janeiro, at 84–85, and DINIZ, Curso de Direito Civil Brasileiro, Responsabilidade Civil, 2009, São Paulo, at 84–85 and 67–68.
307. See NADER, Curso de Direito Civil, Responsabilidade Civil, 2014, Rio de Janeiro, at 86–87, and Noronha, Direito das Obrigações, São Paulo, 2010, at 593.
308. STJ, 3ª Turma, AgRg no Ag 477.631/SP, Relator Ministro Carlos Alberto Menezes Direito, DJ. 31.03.2003, p. 224. Brasília.
309. STJ, 4ª Turma, REsp 183.508/RJ, Relator Ministro Sálvio de Figueiredo Teixeira, DJ. 10.06.2002, p. 212, Brasília; STJ, 2ª Turma, REsp 487.749/RS, Relatora Ministra Eliana Calmon, DJ. 12.05.2003, p. 298. Brasília.
310. See RESEDÁ, A Função Social do Dano Moral, 2009, São José, at 214–219.
311. See BATTESINI, Novos Horizontes no Estudo da Responsabilidade Civil no Brasil, 2011, São Paulo, at 258–260, and TARTUCE, in: RODRIGUES JUNIOR, MAMEDE e ROCHA, Responsabilidade Civil Contemporânea, 2011, São Paulo, at 591–592.

given by the extension of the harm," the 2002's Brazilian Civil Code contains normative dispositions that, expressly establishes the reduction of the damages proportionally to the harm. Regarding to the value of the damage's reduction in relation to the harm, considering the author's and victim fault's degree, the sole paragraph of the Article 944 of the Civil Code establishes that "if there is excessive disproportion between the fault's degree and the harm, the judge can reduce equitably the damages." As for the reduction of the value of the damages in relation to the harm considering the concurrent fault's degree between the victim and the author, the Article 945 of the Civil Code of 2002 established that "if the victim has concurred faulty to the harmful event, his/her damage will be given taking into account his/her fault's degree facing the harm's authors."

217. In reality, the notion of fault can be considered fundamental to the establishment of the imputation nexus, constituting the main principle that defines the Civil Liability. More than that, the fault's degree from the author and from the victim develops important roles in the quantification of the value of damages. In this sense, while synthesizing the results of an comparative study developed by the European Centre of Tort Law and Insurance Law, Unification of Tort Law: Fault, Widmer[312] register that the majority of legal systems do some type of faults graduation, either the "great negligence versus minimum negligence, passing through stages like 'medium' and 'simple' negligence to the lesser degree, the almost imperceptive fault (lighter fault)," highlighting that the "fault's degrees" develop roles in the "estimation of harms," without casting aside the "all or nothing principle fallowed by almost every system." There is a certain sense, in a road back to the traditional classification according to the faults degrees, originated from Roman law, and it could be qualified as: great fault, light fault and lighter fault. It is considered as great fault, when there is an extreme negligence from the part of the agent, not predicting something predictable to the most common man. It is considered light fault, when there was medium diligence, while the harm could be avoided by an ordinary attention. Finally, it is considered lighter fault, when it is committed due a preventive conduct that transcends the medium standard, and the harm was caused by a lack of an extraordinary attention.[313]

218. Therefore, considering the Brazilian system of torts, it is admitted the equitable reduction of damages in relation to the harm, in the terms of the paragraph of the Article 944, when there is an excessive disproportion between the fault's degree between author and victim regarding the harm, or when is produced a meaningful harm from a conduct qualified as being a lighter fault. Furthermore, it is admitted an equitable reduction of damages regarding the harm, in the terms of Article 945, when the victim has concurred faulty to the harmful event, being the idea of the

312. See WIDMER, Unification of Tort Law: Fault, 2005, The Hague, at 353.

313. See DINIZ, Curso de Direito Civil Brasileiro, Responsabilidade Civil, 2009, São Paulo, at 44, and CALIXTO, A Culpa na Responsabilidade Civil, Estrutura e Função, 2008, Rio de Janeiro, at 119.

victim's fault's degree associated to its qualification as lighter, light or great fault, facing the author's own fault's degree.[314]

§5. Methods of Payment

I. Lump Sum

219. The harm's repairing can be specific, in species or *in natura*, making the reconstitution of the situation prior to the harm, or can be equivalent, through the delivery of pecuniary values to the victim. According to Article 947 of Brazilian Civil Code of 2002, the harm usually must be compensated in kind; however, "if the debtor cannot fulfill the debt in the adjusted specie, it will be substituted by its value in current currency." In fact, the reparation by equivalency with the payment of a lump sum for all harms is the most common method of payment. In practical terms, by deciding the legal process the judge decides an amount in money, specifying a quote destined to the compensation of the harm, comprehending the emergent harms and profit loss, and moral harms.

II. Annuities

220. According to Article 950 of Brazilian Civil Code of 2002, compensation through money annuities is the regular remedy to be chosen if, in consequence of injury to body or health, the earning capacity of the injures person is destroyed or impaired. In short, annuities are fixed in judgments, until the prospective time of retirement. In the terms of Article 950, sole paragraph, the victim may demand that the damages will be paid in one quota (lump sum). Another hypothesis of compensation is through of monetary annuities, which is the payment of nurturing values to the legal dependents of the victim that deceased in accident, hypothesis predicted in Article 948, II, of the Civil Code. In both cases, the annuities can be diminished or maximized according to the social and economic circumstances of the annuities beneficiaries.

III. Others

221. The Brazilian system of torts let, in determined situations, the damages to be paid through the performance of specific acts destined to the mitigation of the harm's consequences. It is the case of public disclosure in cases of injury, defamation or calumny (Article 953 of the Civil Code), that can be done by publishing a note in the communication means.[315]

314. See BATTESINI, Novos Horizontes no Estudo da Responsabilidade Civil no Brasil, 2011, São Paulo, at 263–264.
315. See FARIAS, BRAGA NETTO & ROSENVALD, Novo Tratado de Responsabilidade Civil, 2015, São Paulo, at 312–313.

Chapter 4. Personal Injury and Death

§1. Pecuniary Losses

222. In the case of the victim suffer another offense to health that outcomes temporarily or permanently in a reduction in his/her work's capacity, in the terms of the Article 949 of the 2002's Brazilian Civil Code, the damages will consist in the payment of the treatment expenses (medical, chirurgical, residence, exams, remedies, and other expenditures related to the harm's treatment), of profit losses until the end of the treatment, aside other harms that the victim may have suffered. If, the offense results in defect by which the victim cannot exercise his/her job or work or diminishes her/her work capacity, in the terms of Article 950, the damages will include the payment for pension, that will be fixed in values correspondent to the importance of the work which the victim has been disabled or in the proportion of the reduction of his/her labor capacity.[316]

223. In case of victims' death, in the terms of Article 948, I and II, of the Civil Code, the damages will consist in the payment of: treatment expenses, in the case of the victim does not decease immediately; expenses with the funeral and family mourning (mourning services, cremation, body preparation, etc...); as well as the pension to people who the victim owed nurturing, taking in account the probable life span of the victim. The pension will be fixed in two-thirds of the victims' earnings, given the assumption that one-third would be necessary for his/her living costs, if he/she was alive.[317] By jurisprudential construction, the pension is due to the parents in case of a child decease[318] which has been granted considering the victim expected life span from the death date,[319] it is adopted as reference the math table of average life span from the Brazilian population given by the Brazilian Institute of Geography and Statistics (Instituto Brasileiro de Geografia e Estatística).[320] In addition, the pension due to the children in case of parents' decease ends at the 25th birthday from the beneficiary, given the presuppose that in this age he/she will have achieved his/her academic formation (including university).[321]

316. See SENA, in: RODRIGUES JUNIOR, MAMEDE e ROCHA, Responsabilidade Civil Contemporânea, 2011, São Paulo, at 690–691, and CAVALIERI FILHO, Programa de Responsabilidade Civil, 2012, São Paulo, at 122–123.
317. See NANNI, in: Rodrigues JUNIOR, MAMEDE e ROCHA, Responsabilidade Civil Contemporânea, 2011, São Paulo, at 642–655, and CAVALIERI FILHO, Programa de Responsabilidade Civil, 2012, São Paulo, at 121–122.
318. STJ, súmula nº 491. Brasília.
319. STJ, 3ª Turma, AgRg no REsp 1.524.765/PE, Relator Ministro Paulo de Tarso Sanseverino, DJe. 07.10.2015. Brasília.
320. The Brazilian expected life span for a newborn Brazilian in 2014 was estimated to be 75 years and two months. See Instituto Brasileiro de Geografia e Estatística - IBGE, Tábua Completa de Mortalidade, Brasília, 2015. Available at pesquisa.in.gov.br.
321. STJ, 3ª Turma, AgRg no REsp 1.529.730/RJ, Relator Ministro Ricardo Villa Bôas Cueva, DJe. 31.08.2015. Brasilia.

§2. NON-PECUNIARY LOSSES

224. In case of body and health injury, according Article 186 combined with Article 927 of the Brazilian Civil Code, in addition to pecuniary losses, the victim can demand monetary compensation for non-pecuniary losses or moral damages.[322] It is, in essence, the compensation for suffering, physical or psychical pain, inflicted to the victim, developing the "satisfaction of the victim's function," aimed to ameliorate the consequences of the harmful event faced by the victim.[323]

225. Prevails in Brazilian doctrine and jurisprudence the comprehension that the moral damages fulfill a double function: by the victim's perspective, it acts as compensation, fulfilling a satisfactory function; and by the author's side, it acts as a punishment for the harm caused the sanctionary function. As for the mixed character of the moral damages, it is emblematic the manifestation of Pereira:

> in the reparation for moral harms, are encompassed in two reasons or two related causes: I) the punishment of the offender by the offense to a legal food of the victim, due its immateriality; II) to give to the offended a sum that is not a *premium doloris*, but a mean to achieve a satisfaction of any nature, either intellectual or moral, or even material.[324]

The double function of the moral damages is crystallized by the Superior Court of Justice (Superior Tribunal de Justiça), that attributes to the institute: a function to repay the affected party by the harms suffered, aiming to minimize the victim's pain and; the pedagogic function, aimed for the agent of the harmful act, to avoid similar events to occur in the future.[325]

226. In the scenario of the Brazilian torts system, the fixation of the moral damages amount in cases of injury to body and health is a task relied to the judiciary. As consolidated by the rational of the Superior Court of Justice (Superior Tribunal de Justiça), the moral damages are not subject of tabling,[326] it must be object of equitable appreciation of the judiciary. In the terms coined by Cavalieri Filho, "the principle of reasonable logics must be the compass to north the judge. It is reasonable what is sensate, demure, moderated; what retains a certain proportionality. Reasonability is a criterion that allows balancing means and ends, causes and consequences, to reach the decision's logic."[327] The Superior Court of Justice has

322. In the terms of the Súmula nº 37 of the Superior Court of Justice (Superior Tribunal de Justiça): "are commutable the damages by material and moral harms originated by the same fact."
323. See ANDRADE, Dano Moral e Indenização Punitiva: Os Punitive Damages na Experiência da Common Law e na Perspectiva do Direito Brasileiro, 2009, Rio de Janeiro, at 149-150, and RESEDÁ, A Função Social do Dano Moral, 2009, São José, at 178–179.
324. See PEREIRA, Responsabilidade Civil, 2012, Rio de Janeiro, at 413.
325. STJ, 1ª Turma, REsp 1.109.303/RS, Relator Ministro Luiz Fux, DJe. 05.08.2009. Brasília.
326. STJ, súmula nº 281. Brasília.
327. See CAVALIERI FILHO, Programa de Responsabilidade Civil, 2012, São Paulo, at 98.

admitted as a reasonable value in case of victim's death, the fixation of moral damages in a scale between 100 to 500 minimum wages, values among 22,000 to 110,000 American dollars or 19.800 to 98.900 Euros,[328] according to the circumstances of the concrete case.[329]

328. The minimum wage in Brazil in February 2016, was 880 reais, equivalent to 220 American dollars of 198 euros at the time's exchange rate.

329. STJ, 1ª Turma, REsp 704.873/SP, Relatora Ministra Denise Arruda, DJ. 02.08.2007, p. 346 – indemnity of 100 minimum wages for her husband's murder in prison; STJ, 3ª Turma, REsp 329.979/MG, Relator Ministro Carlos Alberto Menezes Direito, DJ. 22.04.2002, p. 202 – indemnity of 200 minimum wages for his son's death in hospital; STJ, 1ª Turma, REsp 799.939/MG, Relator Ministro Luiz Fux, DJ. 30.08.2007 – compensation of 300 minimum wages for young death in a traffic accident with school bus; STJ, 4ª Turma, REsp 1.279.173/SP, Relator Ministro Paulo de Tarso Sanseverino, DJe. 09.04.2013 – compensation 400 minimum wages for young death falling from train, and; STJ, 4ª Turma, REsp 223.545/SP, Relator Ministro Cesar Asfor Rocha, DJ. 26.06.2000, p. 179 – indemnity of 500 minimum wages for death of wife / mother in a traffic accident.

Chapter 5. Various Damages (Property)

227. In cases of property damages, the reparation must be specific, in species or in natura, being composed by the reconstitution of the factual prior situation regarding the harmful event, or to the equivalent delivery of pecuniary values to the victim. According to Article 947 of Brazilian Civil Code of 2002, the harm usually must to be compensated in kind; however, "if the debtor does not be able to fulfill the debt in the adjusted nature, it will be substituted by its value in current currency." In fact, the equivalency compensation, with the payment given in money is proper to originate a state of reality equivalent to the moment prior to the harm; it is the most common way of reparation to property harms.[330]

228. The patrimonial losses calculation to the compensatory ends is done considering the Market values, either of the affected goods or the goods and services necessary to repair the harmed ones. If the object is lost or fully destroyed, the amount will be determined considering the current replacement value. For instance, in the case of motor vehicles, it is common the use of a table made by the Foundation Institute of Economics Researches (Fundação Instituto de Pesquisas Econômicas – FIPE), which express the average prices in vehicles used in the national market, serving as a guide to evaluations.[331] If the object is partially destroyed, the amount will be determined considering the costs of repair. Once more, considering the cases of vehicles as reference, the size of the amount necessary to fix the vehicle, generally, is done through the presentation of three quotations done by trustworthy and capacitated firms, adopting the lesser value.[332]

330. See NADER, Curso de Direito Civil, Responsabilidade Civil, 2014. Rio de Janeiro, at 84–85, and RIZZARDO, Responsabilidade Civil, 2007, Rio de Janeiro, at 53–56.
331. See FUNDAÇÃO INSTITUTO DE PESQUISAS ECONÔMICAS, Tabela de Veículos Automotores. Available at http://veiculos.fipe.org.br.
332. See NADER, Curso de Direito Civil, Responsabilidade Civil, 2014, Rio de Janeiro, at 217–218, and RIZZARDO, Responsabilidade Civil, 2007, Rio de Janeiro, at 59–62.

Chapter 6. Interference with Collateral Benefits

§1. Insurance

229. Private insurance is widespread in Brazil, either as first-party insurance or as third party insurance, as voluntary insurance or as mandatory insurance. Wide are the modalities of insurance available in Brazil, with highlights to the patrimonial, personal, transportation and motor vehicles insurances.[333] A relatively new insurance kind though already very popular, especially in the health care field, is the civil liability's insurance. With express legal prediction in the Article 787 of 2002's Brazilian Civil Code, the civil liability's insurance is an institute from which the insured hires the economic subrogation by the securer for the obligations derived by his/her eventual consideration as liable for his/her actions during determined activity.[334] Among the modalities of mandatory insurance, the motor vehicles mandatory insurance, DPVAT, is highlighted. The vehicle's owner, by expanding or renewing the vehicle's license must contract the stipulated insurance to favor third parties as potential accident's victims.

230. In cases of civil liability, in brief, usually, by being demanded by the victim, the insured reaches the insurer, which will be obliged to pay damages to the victim in the limits and conditions contracted by the insurance contract. According to the Article 781 of the Civil Code, it can occur the full price of the vehicle damages by the insurance company, in the case it is equal or inferior to the limits of the hired values, or will occur the partial damages for the vehicle by the insurance company, in the case of the cover limit contracted is inferior to the verified harm. In the hypothesis of the partial cover, the insured will respond for the residual value due to the victim. If occur the insolvency of the insurance company, the insured liability is due to the victim. By performing the damages to the victim, the insurance company subrogates itself in the rights and actions that compete to the insured against third parties, in the terms of the Article 786 of the Civil Code.[335] Specifically, regarding the mandatory insurance for the motor vehicle owners – DPVAT, the victim is paid damages directly by the insurance company. If there is a legal dispute, as consolidates by the Superior Court of Justice (Superior Tribunal de Justiça), "the value of the mandatory insurance must be deduced from the legal damages fixated."[336]

§2. Social Security and Medicare

231. Brazil has a wide public system of social insurance, encompassing the health, social assistance, and providential care fields (Article 194 of the Federal

333. The regulation of the insurance markets, the open providence, capitalization and re-insurance in Brazil is made by the Private Insurances Superintendence (Superintendência de Seguros Privados – SUSEP). See www.susep.gov.br.
334. See SCHREIBER, Novos Paradigmas da Responsabilidade Civil, 2009, São Paulo, at 222–223.
335. See DINIZ, Curso de Direito Civil, Responsabilidade Civil, 2009, São Paulo, at 228–233.
336. See Súmula 246 do Superior Tribunal de Justiça. Brasília.

Constitution). In synthesis, the public health services (Article 196 of the Constitution) are universally accessible to the population, being financed by the Brazilian society as a whole and headed jointly by the Union, States and Municipalities, Federated Entities that composes the Sole Health System (*Sistema Único de Saúde - SUS*) (Article 198 of the Federal Constitution). The public services of social assistance (Article 203 of the Constitution) are characterized by the public financing and for being headed jointly for the Union, States and Municipalities to people that may need its services, encompassing children, adolescents, elders, and handicapped care. In completion to the public network, the health and social assistance services are also given by private entities. There is a wide spectrum of private health insurances available.[337] As for the public providence, it contemplates the existence a Special Social Providence Regime for Public Servants (Article 40 of the Federal Constitution) and a General Social Providence Regime for private workers (Article 201 of the Federal Constitution). The Brazilian Providence is featured by its contributive character and mandatory affiliation, encompassing cover for events of sickness, handicap, death, and old age. In addition to the public providence, there are also private providence plans available.[338]

232. The social security has a significant impact on tort law, given that most victims of body injure are compensated for their medical expenses, earning losses, and increased necessities by social security. As for the interface between the civil liability and the public and private health systems, in a nutshell, the medical expenses as the victims' treatments are paid by the public powers and private entities, without damages payment by the harm's agent (negative externality), which is a common ground in traffic accidents, for instance. As for the interface between tort law and the public/private providence system, of wide application is the "principle of accumulation of amounts" of security nature with the compensatory nature.[339] For this topic, is mandatory the acknowledgement of Rizzardo's manifestation, where: "it is one of the most pacified subject in jurisprudence and doctrine, the consolidation, unanimous, of the sum of the providence's as pension, insurance and damages values in accidents of work, with the damages paid by different causes, thus the nature of one does not confuse itself with the other."[340] It is representative, in this particular subject, of labor accidents, the constitutional treatment of the Supreme Federal Court's (Supremo Tribunal Federal). According to the Article 7, XXVIII, the labor accidents insurance, due to the employer, does not excludes damages for he/she is obliged to through intent or fault. In the terms of Sumula 229 of the Supreme Federal Court, "the accident damages payment does not exclude the common rights, in case of intent or great fault of the employer."[341]

---

337. The regulation of the complementary health plans is carried out by the National Health Agency (Agência Nacional de Saúde Suplementar – ANS). See www.ans.gov.br.
338. The insurance market regulation, open providence, capitalization and re-insurance in Brazil is made by the Private Insurance Superintendence (Superintendência de Seguros Privados – SUSEP). See www.susep.gov.br.
339. See GONÇALVES, Responsabilidade Civil, 2006, São Paulo, at 812–813.
340. See RIZZARDO, Responsabilidade Civil, 2007, Rio de Janeiro, at 908.
341. See Súmula 229 do Supremo Tribunal Federal. Brasília.

§3. OTHERS

233. Along with the harmful event, besides the insurance and social security benefits, the victim may receive monetary benefits derived from other sources. In this case, such benefits may result in a reduction of the victim's claim in order to compensate the benefits received from those sources, depending on the courts rational and specific laws applicable to these cases.

Chapter 7. Other Remedies

§1. Restitution (For Unjust Enrichment)

234. The unjust enrichment is object of regulation in the Chapter 4, Title VII – Unilateral Acts, of the Obligations Book of the 2002's Brazilian Civil Code. In the terms of Article 884, "one who, without just cause, enriches him/herself at the cost of other, will be obliged to restitute the undue amount acquired." In essence, the unjust enrichment is a patrimonial advantage acquired by a subject of rights without legal fundament, implying to the subject who earn the patrimonial advantage to compensate the harmed subject. In contraposition to the civil liability, which has by its main finalities to recomposes the patrimonial reduction of a creditor, throughout the reparation of harms; the unjust enrichment has by its goal to remove the third party's patrimony undue credits, restituting them to the creditor.[342] In brief, by considering the theme of damages evaluation, it is tight the line between the patrimonial compensation from the unjust enrichment of the victim. Situation that has relevance in moral damages, thus the doctrine and jurisprudence in Brazil admits that, in addition to the compensatory function, the quantification of the damages should consider the punitive and pedagogic function.[343]

§2. Injunctive Relief

235. The injunctive relief is the object of Title II, Book V – Provisory Remedy, from the Brazilian Procedure Civil Code of 2015, and it can be conceded by the Judiciary, in the terms of Article 300 of the Procedure Code, "when there are elements that fundaments the probability of a right and danger of harm or risk to the useful result of the process." Even that the 2002's Brazilian Civil Code does not contemplate specific situations of civil liability that may justify the urgent remedy, it can be used by illicit acts victims in situations in which is necessary for the Judiciary to order a person to do something or to stop doing something connected with a harmful situation.

§3. Punitive Damages

236. In synthesis, under the rules of Brazilian tort law, damages have a compensatory nature. The objective of the tort law system is to put the victim in the same position he would be if the illicit act had not taken place. Therefore, as occurs in the great majority of civil law tradition countries, by the lack of specific prediction, the

342. See NORONHA, Direito das Obrigações, 2010, São Paulo, at 443–444, and COELHO, Curso de Direito Civil, Responsabilidade Civil, 2005, São Paulo, at 243–244.

343. See §2. Non-pecuniary losses, Chapter 4. Personal Injury and Death, Part VI. Remedies.

punitive damages are not admitted in Brazilian tort law.[344] In this sense, as externs Calixto:[345]

> the base-norm in the harm's reparation theme still lies in the Article's 944, of the Civil Code's caput, according to "the damages are given by the extension of the harm. It can be "admitted, though, the reduction of the damages values... on the other hand, it will be admitted the raise of compensation values, as a deterrence to the offender's behavior in the case of specific legislations – which is not present in the current Civil Code.

237. Gradually, though, under influence of the common law's experience, the punitive damages theme has been debated under the Brazilian tort law's field. There is a consistent national doctrine that defends the application of the punitive damages through the moral damages, casting its fundaments from the constitutional principles, comprehension that has been implicitly being accepted by jurisprudence.[346] In this sense, as states Andrade:[347]

> the Brazilian Civil Code does not contemplate expressively the application of damages in their punitive nature. To the contrary, the general rule is given by the Article 944 that established that the extension of the harm gives the limits to the damages … Independent of any legal prediction, the punitive damages in moral damages is applicable in our legal ordainment, which funds themselves in the constitutional principles.

344. See BATTESINI, Negligence, Hand Formula and Compensation, 2013. New York, SSRN, at 14–15, http://ssrn.com/abstract=1988935.
345. See CALIXTO, A Culpa na Responsabilidade Civil, Estrutura e Função, 2008, Rio de Janeiro, at 309–310.
346. See §2. Non-pecuniary losses, Ch. 4. Personal Injury and Death, Part VI. Remedies.
347. See ANDRADE, Dano Moral e Indenização Punitiva: Os Punitive Damages na Experiência da Common Law e na Perspectiva do Direito Brasileiro, 2009, Rio de Janeiro, at 236–237.

Selected Bibliography

General Bibliography

THE ECONOMIST (2012). Democracy Index Economist Intelligence Unit. Visited in June 21, 2013.

THE ECONOMIST (2010). Democracy Index Economist Intelligence Unit. Visited in June 21, 2013.ESTADO DE SÃO PAULO, "A vitória de Dilma." Available at http://www.estadao.com.br/estadaodehoje/20101102/not_imp633577,0.php.

G1. "Manifestações contra o Governo Dilma ocorrem pelo País," Available at http://g1.globo.com/politica/noticia/2016/03/manifestacoes-contra-governo-dilma-ocorrem-pelopais.html.

Observatório Nacional de Segurança Viária – ONSV, Retrato da Segurança Viária no Brasil, Brasília, 2014. Available at http://onsv.org.br.

PORTAL TERRA Governo brasileiro é pressionado por históricos protestos (June 21, 2013). Available at http://noticias.terra.com.br/brasil/governo-brasileiro-e-pressionado-por-historicos.protestos,f614e49fccf5f310VgnCLD2000000ec6eb0aRCRD.html.

AGGIO, Alberto. Política e sociedade no Brasil, 1930-1964. São Paulo: Annablume, 2002.

BARBOSA, Rui. A raiz das coisas: o Brasil no mundo. São Paulo: Civilização Brasileira, 2008.

BARCELLOS, Marta & AZEVEDO, Simone. Histórias do Mercado de Capitais no Brasil. Campus Elsevier 2011. São Paulo.

BOXER, Charles R. IMPÉRIO MARÍTIMO PORTUGUÊS – 1415–1825. São Paulo: Companhia das Letras, 2011.

BRAD SHAW FOUNDATION, "Journey of mankind." Retrieved November 17, 2009. Available at http://www.bradshawfoundation.com/stephenoppenheimer/index.php.

BUENO, Eduardo. Brasil uma História. São Paulo: Editora Ática, 2004.

CUNHA, Manuela Carneiro. História dos Índios no Brasil. São Paulo: Companhia das Letras, 1992.

ETHNOLOGUE, Languages of the World. Available at http://www.ethnologue.com/country/br and CENSUS, IBGE. Available at http://censo2010.ibge.gov.br/apps/atlas.

FAUSTO, Boris e DEVOTO Fernando J. Devoto. História do Brasil. São Paulo: Sebo Avalovara, 2004.

FILIPPI, Eduardo Ernesto. Evolução econômica e institucional do setor primário no Brasil: em direção ao desenvolvimento rural? Maputo, 2006.

GASPARI, Elio. A ditadura escancarada. São Paulo: Companhia das Letras, 2002.

GOMES, Marco Antônio Ferreira, FRIZOLA, Heloisa Ferreira and SPADOTTO, Cláudio. Revista Do Departamento De Geografia, 18 (2006) 67-74. "CLASSIFICAÇÃO DAS ÁREAS DE RECARGA DO SISTEMA AQÜÍFERO GUARANI NO BRASIL EM DOMÍNIOS PEDOMORFOAGROCLIMÁTICOS – SUBSÍDIO AOS ESTUDOS DE AVALIAÇÃO DE RISCO DE CONTAMINAÇÃO DAS ÁGUAS SUBTERRÂNEAS." CLASSIFICAÇÃO DAS ÁREAS DE RECARGA DO SISTEMA AQÜÍFERO GUARANI NO BRASIL EM DOMÍNIOS PEDOMORFOAGROCLIMÁTICOS – SUBSÍDIO AOS ESTUDOS DE AVALIAÇÃO DE RISCO DE CONTAMINAÇÃO DAS ÁGUAS (n.d.): n. pag. Oct. 2005. Web. Available at https://www.embrapa.br/busca-de-publicacoes/-/publicacao/15909/classificacao-das-areas-de-recarga-do-sistema-aquifero-guarani-no-brasil-em-dominios-pedomorfoagroclimaticos---subsidios-aos-estudos-de-avaliacao-do-risco-de-contaminacao-das-aguas-subterraneas.

GUTTENBERG, Pacheco Lopes Junior. "The Sino-Brazilian Principles in a Latin American and BRICS Context: The Case for Comparative Public Budgeting Legal Research." Wisconsin International Law Journal. 13 May, 2015. Retrieved 6 June, Madison, 2015.

HERNANI, Donato. Dicionário das Batalhas Brasileiras. São Paulo: Ibrasa, 1996.

HOLANDA, Sérgio Buarque, CAMPOS, Pedro Moacyr and FAUSTO, Boris. História geral da civilização brasileira. São Paulo: Difusão Européia.

IBGE, *Instituto Brasileiro de Geografia e Economia* (Brazilian Institute for Geografic and Economic Data). 2010 IBGE's Census. Available at www.ibge.gov.br.

LEAL, Victor Nunes. Coronelismo, Enxada e Voto: o município e o sistema representativo no Brasil. São Paulo: Companhia das Letras, 1949.

LYRA, Heitor. História de Dom Pedro II (1825–1891): Ascenção (1825–1870) 1. História de Dom Pedro II (1825–1891): Fastígio (1870–1880) 2. História de Dom Pedro II (1825–1891): Declínio (1880–1891) 3 (in Portuguese). Belo Horizonte: Itatiaia, 1977.

LUSTOSA, Isabel. D. Pedro I - um herói sem nenhum caráter. São Paulo: Cia. das Letras, 2006.

MELLO, Christiane Figueiredo Pagano. "Forças Militares no Brasil Colonial" E-papers 2009 ISBN 9788576502050. Rio de Janeiro. Available at http://www.e-papers.com.br/produtos.asp?codigo_produto=1667.

MENDONÇA, Daniel. Tancredo Neves – Da Distensão à Nova República. Santa Cruz do Sul: Edunisc, 2004.

MERCOSUR. Acerca del MERCOSUR. Available at www.mercosur.int.

MOSHER, Jeffrey C. Political Struggle, Ideology, and State Building: Pernambuco and the Construction of Brazil, 1817-1850. 2008 [S.l.]: U of Nebraska Press. Lincoln.

MSN. ENCARTA. "Plant and Animal Life." MSN. Archived from the original on 31 October 2009. Retrieved 12 June, 2008.

______ "Environmental Issues." MSN. Archived from the original on 31 October 2009. Retrieved 12 June, 2008.

PAIVA, Denise. Era outra história: política social do governo Itamar Franco 1992–1994. Juiz de Fora, Editora UFJF, 2009.

PENNA, Lincoln de Abreu. O progresso da ordem: O florianismo e a construção da República. Rio de Janeiro, 2008.
PRADO, Maria Ligia. A Formação das Nações Latino-Americanas. Campinas, 1986.
RODRIGUEZ, José Honório & Ricardo A.S. Seitenfus. Leda Boechat Rodrigues. História Diplomática do Brasil, 1995. São Paulo.
SEITENFUS, Ricardo AS. "2.2," A entrada do Brasil na Segunda Guerra Mundial. Porto Alegre: EdiPUCRS, 2000.
SKIDMORE, Thomas. História Geral. Recife: Livraria Progresso Sebo 2003.
VIANNA, Hélio. "História do Brasil: período colonial, monarquia e república. 15. ed. São Paulo: Melhoramentos, 1994.

Legal Bibliography

ACCIARRI, Hugo. La Relación de Causalidad y las Funciones del Derecho de Daños. Buenos Aires: Abeledo Perrot, 2009.
ANDRADE, André Gustavo Corrêa de. Dano moral e indenização punitiva: os punitive damages na experiência do common law e na perspectiva do direito brasileiro. 2ª ed. Rio de Janeiro: Lumen Juris, 2009.
BATTESINI, Eugênio. Direito e Economia, Novos Horizontes no Estudo da Responsabilidade Civil no Brasil. São Paulo: LTr, 2011.
BATTESINI, Eugênio. Negligence, Hand Formula, and Compensation (January 20, 2012). Available at SSRN: http://ssrn.com/abstract=1988935 or http://dx.doi.org/10.2139/ssrn.1988935.
BATTESINI, Eugênio. Comparison of Tort Law Systems from the Perspective of Economic Efficiency: Brazilian Civil Code, Principles of European Law and Restatements of the Law (April 17, 2015). Available at SSRN: http://ssrn.com/abstract=2595790 or http://dx.doi.org/10.2139/ssrn.2595790.
BATTESINI, Eugênio. Tort Law and Economic Development: Strict Liability in Legal Practice, ALACDE, 2015. Available at ALACDE: http://laijle.alacde.org/journal/vol1/iss1/2.
BENJAMIN, Antônio Hermann. O Código de Defesa do Consumidor, 10 ª ed. Rio de Janeiro: Forense Universitária, 2011.
BITTAR, Carlos Alberto. Responsabilidade civil: teoria e prática. 2. ed. Rio de Janeiro: Forense Universitária, 1990.
BORGES, Gustavo. "Erro Médico nas Cirurgias Plásticas." São Paulo: Atlas, 2014.
BOUKAERT, Boudewijn and DE GEEST, Gerrit (org.). Encyclopedia of Law and Economics. Cheltenham: Edward Elgar, 2009.
CALIXTO, Marcelo Junqueira. A Culpa na Responsabilidade Civil, Estrutura e Função. Rio de Janeiro: Renovar, 2008.
CAMPINHO, Sérgio. O Direito da Empresa à luz no Novo Código Civil, 11ª ed. Rio de Janeiro: Renovar, 2010.
CANOTILHO, J.J. Gomes; MENDES, Gilmar Ferreira; SARLET, Ingo Wolfgang; STRECK, Lenio (Coord.). Comentários à Constituição do Brasil. São Paulo: Saraiva/Almedina, 2013.

Selected Bibliography

CAVALIERI FILHO, Sérgio. Programa de Responsabilidade Civil, 9ª ed. São Paulo: Atlas, 2010.

COELHO, Fábio Ulhoa. Curso de Direito Civil – Responsabilidade Civil, 2ª ed. São Paulo: Saraiva, 2005.

COELHO, Inocêncio Martires, in CANOTILHO, J. J. Gomes; MENDES, Gilmar Ferreira; SARLET, Ingo Wolfgang; STRECK, Lenio (Coord.). Comentários à Constituição do Brasil. São Paulo: Saraiva/Almedina, 2013.

COOTER, Robert and ULEN, Thomas. Law and Economics, 5ª ed. Pearson Education, 2008. Boston.

CRUZ, Gisela Sampaio da. O Problema do Nexo Causal na Responsabilidade Civil. Rio de Janeiro: Renovar, 2005.

DAM, Cees Van. European Tort Law. Oxford: Oxford University Press, 2006.

DIAS, José de Aguiar. Cláusula de não-indenizar. 4ª ed. Rio de Janeiro: Forense, 1980.

DIAS, José de Aguiar. Da Responsabilidade Civil. 11ª ed. Renovar, 2006. Rio de Janeiro.

DINIZ, Maria Helena. Curso de direito civil brasileiro. V. 7. Responsabilidade Civil. 19. ed. São Paulo: Saraiva, 2009.

DIREITO, Carlos Alberto Menezes and CAVALIERI FILHO, Sérgio. Comentários ao Novo Código Civil, V. XIII, Da Responsabilidade Civil, Das Preferências e Privilégios Creditórios. 2ª ed. Rio de Janeiro: Forense, 2007.

FACHINI NETO, Eugênio. Da Responsabilidade Civil no Novo Código. In. SARLET, Ingo W. (org.). O Novo Código Civil e a Constituição. 2ª ed. Porto Alegre: Livraria do Advogado, 2006.

FARIAS, Cristiano Chaves; BRAGA NETTO, Felipe Peixoto; and ROSENVALD, Nelson. Novo Tratado de Responsabilidade Civil. São Paulo: Atlas, 2015.

FIÚZA, César Augusto de Castro. Direito civil. Curso completo. 14. ed. Belo Horizonte: Del Rey, 2010.

GAMA, Guilherme Calmon Nogueira. Critérios de Valoração da Indenização, Obrigação Indeterminada e Substituição do Valor da Indenização. In: RODRIGUES JUNIOR, Otávio Luiz, MAMEDE, Gladston, and ROCHA, Maria Vital. Responsabilidade Civil Contemporânea. São Paulo: Atlas, 2011.

GONÇALVES, Carlos Roberto. Responsabilidade Civil. 9ª ed. São Paulo: Saraiva, 2006.

GONÇALVES, Carlos Roberto. Direito Civil Brasileiro, vol. 4. São Paulo: Saraiva, 2007.

HART, H.L.A. & HONORÉ, Tony. Causation in the Law. Oxford: Oxford University Press.

KOCH, Bernhard A. and KOZIOL, Helmut. Comparative Conclusions. In KOCH, Bernhard A. and KOZIOL, Unification of Tort Law: Strict Liability. The Hague: Kluwer Law International, 2002. Principles of European Tort Law, v. 6, European Centre of Tort Law and Insurance Law.

LIMA, Alvino. A responsabilidade civil pelo fato de outrem. Rio de Janeiro: Ed. Borsoi, 1972.

LISBOA, Roberto Senise. Manual de Direito Civil, vol. 2 – Obrigações e Responsabilidade Civil, 3ª ed. São Paulo: Revista dos Tribunais, 2004.

LÔBO, Paulo. Direito Civil – Contratos. São Paulo: Saraiva, 2011.

MELLO, Marcos Bernardes. Teoria do Fato Jurídico – Plano da Existência, 12ª ed. São Paulo: Saraiva, 2003.

MIRAGEM, Bruno. Abuso do Direito = Proteção da Confiança e Limite ao Exercício das Prerrogativas Jurídicas no Direito Privado. Rio de Janeiro: Forense, 2009.

MIRANDA, Francisco C. Pontes de. Atualização: Vilson Rodrigues Alves. Tratado de direito privado. Campinas: Bookseller Editora, 2003.

MORAES, Maria Celina Bodin de. Danos à pessoa humana: uma leitura civil- constitucional dos danos extrapatrimoniais. São Paulo: Renovar, 2003.

NADER, Paulo. Curso de Direito Civil, vol. 7 – Responsabilidade Civil, 5ª ed. Rio de Janeiro: Forense, 2014.

NANNI, Giovanni Ettore. Indenização e Homicídio. In RODRIGUES JUNIOR, Otávio Luiz, MAMEDE, Gladston, and ROCHA, Maria Vital. Responsabilidade Civil Contemporânea. São Paulo: Atlas, 2011.

NORONHA, Fernando. Direito das Obrigações, 3ª ed. São Paulo: Saraiva, 2010.

NOVO CÓDIGO CIVIL BRASILEIRO, Lei nº 10.406, de 10 de janeiro de 2002: Estudo Comparativo com o Código de 1916, Constituição Federal, Legislação Codificada e Extravagante. 4ª ed. São Paulo: Revista dos Tribunais, 2004.

PAULA, Carolina Bellini Arantes. As excludentes de Responsabilidade Civil Objetiva. São Paulo: Atlas, 2007.

PASTOR, Santos. Derecho de Daños. In. SPECTOR, Horacio (org.). Elementos de Análisis Económico del Derecho. Buenos Aires: Rubinzal-Culzoni Editores, 2004.

PEREIRA, Caio Mário da Silva. Responsabilidade Civil, 10ª ed. Rio de Janeiro: GZ Editora, 2012.

PINTO, Paulo Mota. Sobre Condição e Causa na Responsabilidade Civil. "Estudos em Homenagem ao Professor Doutor António Castanheira Neves," v. III: Direito Público, Direito Penal e História do Direito. Coimbra: Ed. Coimbra, 2008.

RAZ, Joseph. Practical Reasons and Norms. Oxford: Oxford University Press, 1999.

REALE, Miguel. Diretrizes Gerais sobre o Projeto de Código Civil. In REALE, Estudos de Filosofia e Ciência do Direito. São Paulo: Saraiva, 1978.

REALE, Miguel. Visão Geral do Novo Código Civil. In NOVO CÓDIGO CIVIL BRASILEIRO, Lei nº 10.406, de 10 de janeiro de 2002: Estudo Comparativo com o Código de 1916, Constituição Federal, Legislação Codificada e Extravagante. 4ª ed. São Paulo: Revista dos Tribunais, 2004.

RESEDA, Salomão. A Função Social do Dano Moral. Florianópolis: Conceito Editorial, 2009.

RIZZARDO, Arnaldo. Responsabilidade Civil, 3ª ed. Rio de Janeiro: Forense, 2007.

RODRIGUES, Sílvio. Direito Civil, vol. 4 – Responsabilidade Civil, 19ª ed. São Paulo: Saraiva, 2002.

RODRIGUES JUNIOR, Otávio Luiz, MAMEDE, Gladston, and ROCHA, Maria Vital. Responsabilidade Civil Contemporânea. São Paulo: Atlas, 2011.

SANSEVERINO, Paulo de Tarso Vieira. Princípio da Reparação Integral. São Paulo: Saraiva, 2013.

SANTOLIM, Cesar. Nexo de Causalidade e Prevenção na Responsabilidade Civil, Revista da AJURIS - v. 41 – n. 136 – December 2014. Porto Alegre.

SARLET, Ingo W. (org.). O Novo Código Civil e a Constituição. 2ª ed. Porto Alegre: Livraria do Advogado, 2006.

SENA, Adriana Goulart. Indenização e Perda da Capacidade Laborativa. In RODRIGUES JUNIOR, Otávio Luiz, MAMEDE, Gladston, and ROCHA, Maria Vital. Responsabilidade Civil Contemporânea. São Paulo: Atlas, 2011.

SCHÄFER, Hand-Bernd and OTT, Claus. The Economic Analysis of Civil Law. Cheltenham: Edward Elgar, 2004.

SCHÄFER, Hans-Bernd and Müller-Langer, Strict Liability versus Negligence, in: BOUKAERT, Boudewijn and DE GEEST, Gerrit (org.). Encyclopedia of Law and Economics. Cheltenham: Edward Elgar, 2009.

SCHREIBER, Anderson. Novos Paradigmas da Responsabilidade Civil, da Erosão dos Filtros da Reparação à Diluição dos Danos, 2ª ed. São Paulo: Atlas, 2009.

SEVERO, Sérgio. Tratado da Responsabilidade Pública. São Paulo: Saraiva, 2009.

SHAVELL, Steven. Foundations of Economic Analysis of Law. Cambridge: Harvard University Press, 2004.

SILVA, De Plácido. Vocabulário Jurídico. Rio de Janeiro: Forense, 2008.

SILVA, Wilson Melo da. O dano moral e sua reparação. Rio de Janeiro: Forense, 1969.

SPECTOR, Horácio (org.). Elementos de Análisis Económico del Derecho. Buenos Aires: Rubinzal-Culzoni Editores, 2004.

STOCO, Rui. Tratado de Responsabilidade Civil, 10 ª ed. São Paulo: Revista dos Tribunais, 2014.

TARTUCE, Flávio. Redução Equitativa da Indenização. In RODRIGUES JUNIOR, Otávio Luiz, MAMEDE, Gladston, and ROCHA, Maria Vital. Responsabilidade Civil Contemporânea. São Paulo: Atlas, 2011.

TESTA, Matias Yrigoñen, Daños Punitivos, Análisis Económico del Derecho y Teoría de Juegos. Buenos Aires, 2006.

THEODORO JUNIOR, Humberto. "Comentários ao Novo Código Civil," 2ª ed. Rio de Janeiro: Forense, 2003.

VENTURI, Thaís Goveia Pascoaloto. Responsabilidade Civil Preventiva. São Paulo: Malheiros, 2014.

WALD, Arnold. Direito Civil. V. 7. Obrigações e Contratos. São Paulo: Saraiva, 2009.

WERRO, Franz, PALMER, Vernon V. Strict Liability in European Tort Law: An Introduction. In WERRO, Franz, PALMER, Vernon V. (ed.). The Boundaries of Strict Liability in European Tort Law. Durham: Carolina Academic Press, 2004.

WIDMER, Pierre. Comparative Report on Fault as a Basis of Liability and Criterion of Imputation (Attribution). In WIDMER, Pierre (ed.) Unification of Tort Law: Fault. The Hague: Kluver Law International, 2005. Principles of European Tort Law, v. 10. European Centre of Tort Law and Insurance Law.

ZWEIGERT, Konrad and KÖTZ, Hein. Introducción al Derecho Comparado. Mexico: Oxford University Press, 2002.

Index

The numbers here refer to paragraph numbers.

Index